NEW JOYS OF JELL-O®

BRAND

NEW JOYS OF JELL-O® BRAND

BEEKMAN HOUSE

Pictured on front cover (*clockwise from bottom left*): JELL-O Jigglers (*page 143*), Lemon Cheese Tart (*page 98*), Melon Bubbles (*page 196*) and Elegant Raspberry Chocolate Pie (*page 80*).

Pictured on back cover (*clockwise from top left*): Black Forest Parfaits (*page 26*), Under-the-Sea Salad (*page 148*), JELL-O Jigglers (*page 143*), Carousel Gelatin Cups (*page 136*) and Bunny in a Cloud (*page 139*).

Library of Congress Catalog Card Number: 90-61498

ISBN: 0-517-03071-3

This edition published by Beekman House, Distributed by Crown Publishers, Inc., 225 Park Avenue South, New York, New York 10003

Printed and bound in the United States

8 7 6 5 4 3 2 1

CONTENTS

THE JELL-O COLLECTION

For nearly a century, JELL-O Brand Gelatin and Pudding have been staple ingredients in kitchens all across America. The versatility of these excellent products has made them the perfect "base" for hundreds of recipes.

NEW JOYS OF JELL-O, a magnificent collection of over 220 of the very best JELL-O recipes, can bring these favorites to your home. You'll find traditional crowd pleasers as well as many new creations guaranteed to become family favorites for years to come.

There is an abundance of recipes (beverages, snacks, salads and desserts) for the way you live today. Many can be prepared in 20 minutes or less. In addition, dozens are even simple enough for a child to help with the preparation. No matter what your choice, every recipe is guaranteed to be a success!

This impressive treasury of JELL-O recipes was compiled to provide the millions of JELL-O users with a fabulous collection of JELL-O recipes in one complete source. In response to the countless requests we receive each year for more recipes, the professionals in the General Foods Test Kitchens proudly bring to you NEW JOYS OF JELL-O.

LOOKING BACK

It all began with the famous inventor, Peter Cooper of Tom Thumb Locomotive fame. He was granted the first patent for a gelatin dessert in 1845. Like many inventors, he had several projects going on at once so he had little time to devote to gelatin development. Cooper's gelatin idea literally "sat on the shelf" for 50 years until Pearl B. Wait, a cough medicine manufacturer from LeRoy, New York, decided to do something with it. Wait produced an adaptation of Cooper's idea and his wife coined the name for it—"JELL-O." Production began in 1897 and Wait attempted to market his new product door-to-door. Unfortunately, people were not interested in the newfangled gelatin dessert, so in 1899 Pearl Wait sold the JELL-O business to his neighbor, Orator F. Woodward for $450.

By 1904, the JELL-O business was thriving thanks in part to a successful advertising campaign employing the face of a beautiful little girl named Elizabeth King, who became known as the "JELL-O Girl." The JELL-O Girl helped launch a theme that still holds true today—"You can't be a kid without it."

In 1937, JELL-O pudding was introduced nationally, expanding the JELL-O name beyond gelatin to another dessert that is fun for kids. For over 50 years we have been watching children's faces light up when they dig their spoons into bowls of JELL-O pudding.

Through its 90-plus years, JELL-O has been associated with many famous people. The old JELL-O cookbooks and magazine advertisements were illustrated by noteworthy artists like Norman Rockwell. In radio and television, JELL-O has had a long history of spokespeople reinforcing JELL-O's fun image—Jack Benny, Andy Griffith, and for the past 17 years, Bill Cosby.

Over the years, many products have come and gone, but JELL-O has remained popular for three reasons. It tastes good. It is fun food for kids. It is versatile. JELL-O gelatin and pudding can be used to make hundreds of delicious, imaginative recipes. NEW JOYS OF JELL-O brings you over 200 of these taste-tempting recipes. Some are old favorites and many are new for the nineties . . . the decade of JELL-O's centennial.

Circa 1905

TRICKS OF THE TRADE

Our professionals share their secrets with you—simple additions guaranteed to add pizzazz to any recipe. These foolproof tips, many with step-by-step photos, ensure perfect results every time and the quick, clever garnish ideas are sure to impress family and friends alike.

▪ Gelatin

Making JELL-O Brand Gelatin is easy—you've probably been doing it since you were little. Just follow the package directions and the results are terrific!

The basic directions as written below are also on the package:

- Add 1 cup boiling water to 1 package (4-serving size) gelatin (2 cups water for 8-serving size). Stir until dissolved, about 2 minutes. Add 1 cup cold water (2 cups for 8-serving size). Chill until set.
- JELL-O Brand Sugar Free Gelatin is prepared in the same way. It can be used in any recipe that calls for JELL-O Brand Gelatin.

▪ Some tips for success

- To make a mixture that is clear and uniformly set, be sure the gelatin is <u>completely</u> dissolved in boiling water or other boiling liquid before adding the cold liquid.
- To double a recipe, just double the amounts of gelatin, liquid and other ingredients used except salt, vinegar and lemon juice. For these, use just 1½ times the amount given in the recipe.
- To store prepared gelatin overnight or longer, cover it to prevent drying. Always store gelatin cakes or pies in the refrigerator.

▪ How to speed up chilling time

- Choose the *right container*—a metal bowl or mold rather than glass, plastic or china. Metal chills more quickly and the gelatin will be firm in less time than in glass or plastic bowls. Also, individual servings in small molds or serving dishes will chill more quickly than large servings.

- Speed Set (ice cube method): Dissolve gelatin completely in ¾ cup boiling liquid (1½ cups for 8-serving size). Combine ½ cup water and enough ice cubes to make 1¼ cups (1 cup cold water and enough ice cubes to make 2½ cups for 8-serving size). Add to gelatin, stirring until slightly thickened. Remove any unmelted ice. Pour into dessert dishes or serving bowl. Chill. Mixture will be soft-set and ready to eat in about 30 minutes, firm in 1 to 1½ hours. However, do not use this method if you are going to mold the gelatin.

- Ice bath method: Dissolve gelatin according to package directions. Place bowl of gelatin mixture in larger bowl of ice and water; stir occasionally as mixture chills to ensure even thickening.

Gelatin Chilling Time Chart

In all recipes, for best results, the gelatin needs to be chilled to the proper consistency. Use this chart as a guideline to determine the desired consistency and the approximate chilling time.

When recipe says:	It means gelatin should . . .	It will take about:		Use it for . . .
		Regular set	Speed set*	
"Chill until syrupy"	be consistency of thick syrup	1 hour	3 minutes	glaze for pies, fruits
"Chill until slightly thickened"	be consistency of unbeaten egg whites	1¼ hours	5 to 6 minutes	adding creamy ingredients such as whipped topping, or when mixture will be beaten
"Chill until thickened"	be thick enough so that spoon drawn through it leaves a definite impression	1½ hours	7 to 8 minutes	adding solid ingredients such as fruits or vegetables
"Chill until set but not firm"	stick to the finger when touched and should mound or move to the side when bowl or mold is tilted	2 hours	30 minutes	layering gelatin mixtures
"Chill until firm"	not stick to finger when touched and not mound or move when mold is tilted	Individual molds: at least 3 hours 2- to 6-cup mold: at least 4 hours 8- to 12-cup mold: at least 5 hours or overnight		unmolding and serving

*Speed Set (ice cube method) not recommended for molding.

- Blender method: Place 4-serving size package of gelatin and ¾ cup boiling liquid in blender. (Note: The volume of the 8-serving size package is too large for most blenders.) Cover and blend at low speed until gelatin is completely dissolved, about 30 seconds. Combine ½ cup water and enough ice cubes to make 1¼ cups; add to gelatin. Stir until partially melted. Blend at high speed 30 seconds. Pour into dessert dishes or bowl. Chill until set, at least 30 minutes. Mixture is self-layering and sets with a frothy layer on top, clear layer on bottom.

■ The Secret to Molding Gelatin

The Mold

- Use metal molds, traditional decorative molds and other metal forms, as well. You can use square or round cake pans, fluted or plain tube pans, loaf pans, metal mixing bowls (the nested sets give you a variety of sizes), or metal fruit or juice cans (to unmold, dip can in warm water, then puncture bottom of can and unmold).

- To determine the *volume of the mold,* measure first with water. Most recipes give an indication of the size of the mold needed. For clear gelatin, you need a 2-cup mold for a 4-serving size package of gelatin, and a 4-cup mold for 8-serving size.

- If mold holds less than the amount called for, pour the extra gelatin mixture into a separate dish and serve at another time. Do not use a mold that is too large, since it would be difficult to unmold. Either increase the recipe or use a smaller mold.

- For easier unmolding, spray mold with non-stick cooking spray before filling mold.

The Preparation

- Use less water in preparing gelatin if it is to be molded. For 4-serving size package, use ¾ cup cold water; for 8-serving size, use 1½ cups cold water. (This adjustment has already been made in recipes in this book that are to be molded.) This makes the mold less fragile and makes unmolding much simpler.

- To arrange fruits or vegetables in molds, chill gelatin until thick, then pour gelatin into mold to about ¼-inch depth. Arrange fruits or vegetables in decorative pattern in gelatin. Chill until set but not firm, then pour remaining thickened gelatin over pattern in mold.

The Unmolding

- First, allow gelatin to set until firm, several hours or overnight. Also, chill serving plate or individual plates on which mold will be served.

- Make certain that gelatin is completely firm. It should not feel sticky on top and should not mound or move to the side if mold is tilted.

- Moisten tips of fingers and gently pull gelatin from edge of mold. Or, use a small metal spatula or pointed knife dipped in warm water to loosen top edge.

- Dip mold in warm, not hot, water, just to the rim, for about 10 seconds. Lift from water, hold upright and shake to loosen gelatin. Or, gently pull gelatin from edge of mold.

- Moisten chilled serving plate with cold water; this allows gelatin to be moved after unmolding. Place moistened plate over mold and invert. Shake slightly, then lift off mold carefully. If gelatin doesn't release easily, dip the mold in warm water again for a few seconds. If necessary, move gelatin to center of serving plate.

1. Before unmolding, pull gelatin from edge of mold with moist fingers. Or, run small metal spatula or pointed knife dipped in warm water around edge of gelatin.

2. Dip mold in warm water, just to rim, for 10 seconds.

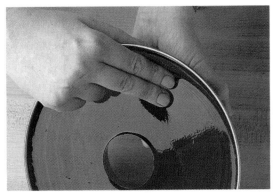

3. Lift from water and gently pull gelatin from edge of mold with moist fingers.

4. Place moistened serving plate on top of mold.

5. Invert mold and plate and shake to loosen gelatin.

6. Gently remove mold and center gelatin on plate.

■ Simple additions to make gelatin special

Fruits and vegetables

Chill gelatin until it is thickened, then fold in ¾ to 1½ cups (1½ to 3 cups for 8-serving size) fruits or vegetables. Do not use fresh or frozen pineapple or kiwifruit or fresh ginger root, papaya, figs or guava; an enzyme in these fruits will prevent the gelatin from setting. These fruits are fine, however, if cooked or canned, because these processes deactivate the enzyme. Canned or fresh fruits should be drained well before adding to gelatin (unless a recipe specifies otherwise). The fruit juice or syrup can be used as part of the liquid called for in recipe.

Carbonated beverages

Substitute cold carbonated beverages, such as club soda, cola, fruit flavor sparkling water, ginger ale, lemon-lime flavor drinks or root beer, for part or all of the cold water.

Fruit juice

Use fruit juice for part of the cold liquid— orange juice, apple juice, cranberry juice, tomato juice or canned pineapple juice. Use boiling fruit juice if replacing boiling water.

Flavored extracts

Add flavoring extracts, such as vanilla, almond, peppermint or rum—just a touch for additional flavor.

Wine or liqueur

Add a little wine or liqueur for a festive touch. Use 2 tablespoons white wine, red wine, sherry or 1 tablespoon creme de menthe or chocolate or fruit flavor liqueur. For 8-serving size package, use 3 tablespoons wine or 1½ tablespoons liqueur.

■ Ways to add extra flair to gelatin

Flake or cube it

Prepare gelatin as usual, reducing cold water to ¾ cup (1½ cups for 8-serving size). Pour into shallow pan and chill until firm, about 3 hours.

- To flake, break gelatin into small flakes with fork or force through a large mesh strainer; pile lightly into dishes, alone or with fruit or whipped topping.

- For cubes, cut gelatin into small cubes, using sharp knife that has been dipped in hot water. To remove cubes from pan, quickly dip pan in warm water and invert onto plastic wrap. Serve in dishes with cream or fruit, if desired.

Layer it

Make layers with different flavors or different types of gelatin mixtures. Chill each layer until set but not firm before adding the next layer; if lower layer is too firm, the layers may slip apart when unmolded. The gelatin should stick to fingers when touched and move gently from side to side when the bowl is tilted. Except for the first layer, the gelatin mixtures should be cool and slightly thickened before being poured into mold; a warm mixture could soften the layer beneath it and cause mixtures to run together.

Tilt it

Fill parfait or any stemmed glasses ½ full with gelatin. Tilt glasses in refrigerator by catching bases of glasses between bars of refrigerator rack and leaning tops of glasses against wall. Chill until set but not firm. Place glasses upright. Fill with additional gelatin as desired. (Use whipped gelatin or another flavor gelatin.) Chill until firm.

Scallop it

Prepare gelatin as usual and pour into sherbet or other dessert glasses. Chill until firm. Use ½ teaspoon measure to scoop out spoonfuls around edges, making scalloped borders. Top with whipped topping, filling scallops. Use scooped-out gelatin for garnish, if desired.

▧ Pudding Pointers

The recipes in this book use both **JELL-O Pudding and Pie Filling,** which requires cooking, and **JELL-O Instant Pudding and Pie Filling,** which is not cooked. These products are not interchangeable in recipes. Be sure to use the product called for in the recipe.

The basic directions as written below are also on the package:

For JELL-O Pudding and Pie Filling:

- Stir contents of 1 package (4-serving size) pudding mix into 2 cups milk (3 cups for 6-serving size) in medium saucepan. Cook and stir over medium heat until mixture comes to full boil. Pudding thickens as it cools. Serve warm or cold.

- Microwave directions: Stir pudding mix with milk in 1½-quart (2-quart for 6-serving size) microwavable bowl. Microwave on HIGH 6 minutes (8 minutes for 6-serving size), stirring every 2 minutes, until mixture comes to boil. Stir well. Chill. Note: Ovens vary; cooking time is approximate. Microwave method not recommended for ovens below 500 watts.

- For pie, cool cooked pudding 5 minutes, stirring twice. Pour into cooled, baked 8-inch pie shell (9-inch highly fluted or 10-inch for 6-serving size). Chill 3 hours.

- JELL-O Lemon Flavor Pie Filling has different directions that call for eggs, sugar and water rather than milk; follow the package directions to make a delicious lemon meringue pie.

For JELL-O Instant Pudding and Pie Filling:

- Pour 2 cups cold milk (3 cups for 6-serving size) into bowl. Add pudding mix. Beat with wire whisk or at lowest speed of electric mixer until well blended, 1 to 2 minutes. Pour immediately into dishes. Pudding will be soft-set, ready to eat in 5 minutes.

- For pies, beat only 1 minute; mixture will be thin. Pour immediately into cooled, baked pie shell (8-inch for 4-serving size, 9-inch for 6-serving size). Chill at least 1 hour. For chocolate, chocolate fudge, milk chocolate or butterscotch flavors, 4-serving size, reduce milk to 1¾ cups; for chocolate and chocolate fudge flavors, 6-serving size, reduce milk to 2⅔ cups.

- Shaker method: Pour cold milk into leakproof 1-quart container (1½-quart container for 6-serving size). Add pudding mix. Cover tightly. Shake vigorously at least 45 seconds. Pour immediately into dessert dishes or serving bowl.

- Fork-Stir method: Place mix in 1-quart bowl. While stirring with fork, gradually add milk. Stir until blended and smooth, about 2 minutes.

- Blender method: Pour cold milk into electric blender. Add pudding mix; cover. Blend at high speed 15 seconds. Pour immediately into dessert dishes or pie shell.

JELL-O Sugar Free Pudding and Pie Filling and Sugar Free Instant Pudding and Pie Filling can be substituted for their respective cooked and instant pudding mixes.

Some tips for success

For JELL-O Pudding and Pie Filling:
- It's best to cook pudding in a heavy saucepan to ensure even heating. Stir pudding mixture constantly as it cooks. Make sure it comes to full boil. The mixture will be thin, but will thicken as it cools.

- For a creamier pudding, stir before serving.

- To cool pudding quickly, place pan of hot pudding in larger pan of ice water; stir frequently until mixture is cooled. Do not use this method for pie filling; the set will not be firm enough.

- For molded pudding recipes, cool cooked pudding 5 minutes, stirring twice; then pour into plain mold or individual custard cups that have been rinsed in cold water. Chill. To unmold, dip mold or cup in hot water.

For JELL-O Instant Pudding and Pie Filling:
- Always use cold milk. Beat pudding mix slowly, not vigorously.

- For best results, use whole or 2% milk. Skim milk, reconstituted nonfat dry milk, light cream or half and half can also be used.

- Always store prepared pudding desserts, snacks and pies in refrigerator.

Pudding Cake Pointers

Adding instant pudding mix to cake mix gives cakes an extra richness and moistness and a homemade taste. For perfect results:

- Follow recipe directions carefully, beating just the time specified and baking at the correct temperature.

- If your cakes usually take less or more time than the time range specified, you might need to have your oven's thermostat checked for accuracy.

- When using a *pudding-included cake mix*, you probably will have to reduce the liquid ingredients. Reduce the water or other liquid by ¼ cup. If sour cream is used rather than water, reduce that by ¼ cup.

- If you live in a *high altitude area*, you're probably used to making baking adjustments. For pudding cakes the usual ingredient adjustments are these: add all-purpose flour to the mix, ¼ to ⅔ cup (more for pudding-included mixes); add about ½ cup water (only ¼ cup if using pudding-included mix); reduce oil to about ¼ cup; and use large eggs. If sour cream is used, that amount should be reduced to about ¼ cup. Any extra ingredients, such as raisins or nuts, should be finely chopped. Use pan sizes recommended in the recipe; grease and flour pans well. When baking, raise temperature about 25° for all but upside-down cakes. Test cake carefully since baking time might be longer.

- If you're using a different size pan than what is called for in the recipe, the baking time will change. A cake baked in smaller pans— 8-inch rather than 9-inch layers, for example—will take slightly longer, 5 to 10 minutes.

- The best tests of doneness: a cake tester inserted in center comes out clean; cake has begun to pull away from sides of pan; or cake springs back when lightly touched.

▨ Show Stoppers

It's those finishing touches that make the professionals' desserts so special. Here are their secrets.

Citrus Zest Strips

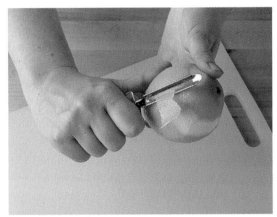

1. Use vegetable peeler to shave off topmost layer from orange peel in wide strips.

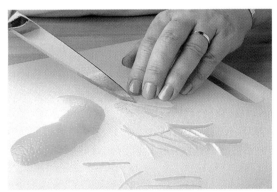

2. With sharp knife, cut peel into narrow strips. Use to flavor desserts or as a garnish.

Citrus Twists

1. With sharp knife, cut orange into thin slices.

2. Cut slit through slices to centers.

3. Twist slices from slits in opposite directions to form twists.

Citrus Fans

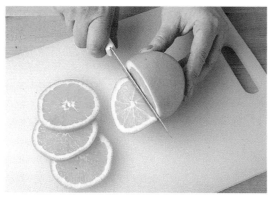

1. With sharp knife, cut orange into thin slices.

2. Stack 3 slices; cut slit through slices to center.

3. Twist slices from slits in opposite directions; twist 3 slices together to give fan effect.

Citrus Curls

Use citrus zester to remove long thin strip of peel from around lemon, lime or orange. Cut into desired length. Roll strip into curl; use as garnish.

Frosted Fruit

Use fresh cranberries or green or red seedless grapes. Dip fruit into 1 lightly beaten egg white. (Note: Use only clean eggs with no cracks in shells.) Hold to permit excess egg white to drain off; roll in sugar in flat plate to coat well. Place on tray covered with waxed paper. Let stand until dry.

Fruit Fans

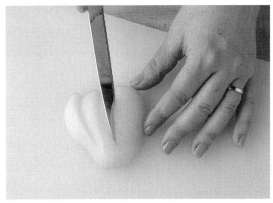

1. With sharp knife, cut drained canned pear halves into thin slices (about 5 or 6), cutting up to, but not through, stem ends. (Use same technique for strawberries.)

2. Hold stem end in place and gently fan out slices from stem before placing on plate for fruit desserts or using as garnish.

Sauce Swirls

1. Spoon Vanilla Sauce (see page 34 for recipe) onto individual dessert plates. Drop small amounts of sauce (chocolate, raspberry or strawberry) or melted chocolate from spoon at intervals over Vanilla Sauce near rim of plate.

2. Draw wooden pick through sauce, swirling through Vanilla Sauce to create design.

Toasted Nuts

Spread nuts in shallow baking pan. Toast at 400°, stirring frequently, 8 to 10 minutes or until golden brown.

Gumdrop Flowers

1. Flatten gumdrops with rolling pin on surface or sheet of waxed paper sprinkled with sugar. Roll until very thin (about ¹⁄₁₆ inch thick), turning frequently to coat with sugar.

2. Hold flattened gumdrop at center; overlap edges slightly to give petal effect, pressing piece together at base to resemble flower. For open blossom, bend gumdrop petals outward from center. Insert small piece of gumdrop in centers with wooden pick, if desired. Use wooden pick to attach flowers to cake if necessary.

Gumdrop Ribbon

1. Line up gumdrops in a row on surface or sheet of waxed paper sprinkled with sugar. Flatten into long strips with rolling pin, turning frequently to coat with sugar.

2. Cut flattened gumdrops with sharp knife into 1-inch strips.

3. To make bow, fold over four strips to form loops of the bow; place on dessert. Then place a small loop in center to cover center of bow. Cut "V"'s at one end of remaining two strips, if desired; place under loops to resemble ends of ribbon.

Whipped Topping Dollops

1. Swirl spoon, held upright, through thawed COOL WHIP Whipped Topping, creating rippled surface on the topping.

2. Dip spoon into rippled topping to scoop up heaping spoonful of topping, maintaining rippled surface.

3. Gently touch spoon onto surface of dessert and release topping gradually onto surface, pulling spoon up into a crowning tip.

Whipped Topping Piping

Insert decorating tip in pastry bag; fill with thawed COOL WHIP Whipped Topping. Fold down top of pastry bag. Holding bag firmly with one hand and squeezing topping down into tip, guide tip around surface to be decorated. Double back topping at intervals for decorative wave effect.

Tinted Coconut

Dilute a few drops of food coloring with ½ teaspoon milk or water; add 1 to 1⅓ cups coconut. Toss with fork until evenly tinted.

Toasted Coconut

Spread coconut in shallow pan. Toast at 350°, stirring frequently, 7 to 12 minutes or until lightly browned. Or toast in microwave oven on HIGH, 5 minutes for 1⅓ cups, stirring several times.

▓ Easy Chocolate Garnishes

Use BAKER'S Semi-Sweet or GERMAN'S Sweet Chocolate.

To melt on range top: Place chocolate in heavy saucepan over *very low* heat; stir *constantly* until just melted.

To melt Semi-Sweet Chocolate in microwave: Place 1 square chocolate, unwrapped, in microwavable dish. Microwave on HIGH 1 to 2 minutes or until almost melted, stirring halfway through heating time. Remove from oven; stir until completely melted. Add 10 seconds for each additional square of chocolate.

To melt GERMAN'S Sweet Chocolate in microwave: Place chocolate, unwrapped and broken in half, in microwavable dish. Microwave on HIGH 1½ to 2 minutes or until almost melted, stirring halfway through heating time. Remove from oven; stir until completely melted.

Chocolate Curls

1. Spread 4 squares melted chocolate with spatula into very thin layer on baking sheet. Chill until firm but still pliable, about 10 minutes.

2. To make curls, slip tip of straight-side metal spatula under chocolate. Push spatula firmly along baking sheet, under chocolate, so chocolate curls as it is pushed. (If chocolate is too firm to curl, let stand a few minutes at room temperature; chill again if it becomes too soft.)

3. Carefully pick up each chocolate curl by inserting wooden pick in center. Lift onto waxed paper-lined baking sheet. Chill until firm, about 15 minutes. Arrange on desserts. (Lift with wooden pick to prevent breakage or melting.)

Chocolate Cutouts

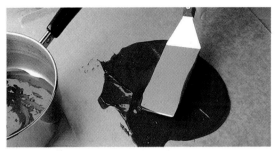

1. Pour melted chocolate onto waxed paper-lined baking sheet; spread to ⅛-inch thickness with spatula. Chill until firm, about 15 minutes.

2. Cut with cookie cutters; immediately lift gently from waxed paper with spatula or knife. Store on waxed paper in refrigerator or freezer. Use to garnish desserts.

Chocolate-Dipped Garnish

Dip fruit, cookies or whole nuts into melted chocolate, covering at least half; let excess chocolate drip off. Arrange on rack or place on waxed paper-lined tray. Let stand or chill until chocolate is firm.

Chocolate Drizzle

1. Place 1 square BAKER'S Semi-Sweet Chocolate in small plastic sandwich bag or self-closing bag. Microwave on HIGH about 1 minute or until chocolate is melted. Fold top of bag tightly and snip off one corner (about ⅛ inch).

2. Hold bag tightly at top and drizzle chocolate through opening over fruit, cookies, cake or pudding.

Shaved Chocolate

Pull vegetable peeler across surface of chocolate square, using short, quick strokes. Sprinkle the shaved chocolate on beverages or desserts.

Carrot Curls

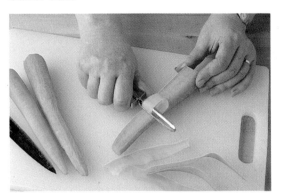

1. With vegetable peeler, cut cleaned carrot into strips the length of the carrot.

2. Twirl strips into curls; fasten with wooden picks. Let stand in ice water until ready to use. Remove wooden picks. Use as garnish on salads or vegetable molds.

Scallion Brushes

1. Clean scallions; remove root tips and trim green stem ends. With sharp knife cut white bulb ends and green stem ends lengthwise into thin slices, keeping center portions intact.

2. Drop sliced scallion into ice water; let stand until ends curl. Use as garnish on salads or vegetable molds.

Circa 1925

QUICK AND EASY

■ Black Forest Parfaits

1 package (8 ounces)
    PHILADELPHIA BRAND Cream
    Cheese, softened
2 cups cold milk
1 package (4-serving size) JELL-O
    Instant Pudding and Pie Filling,
    Chocolate Flavor
1 can (21 ounces) cherry pie filling
1 tablespoon cherry liqueur
½ cup chocolate wafer crumbs

BEAT cream cheese with ½ cup of the milk at low speed of electric mixer until smooth. Add pudding mix and remaining milk. Beat until smooth, 1 to 2 minutes.

MIX together cherry pie filling and liqueur. Reserve a few cherries for garnish, if desired. Spoon ½ of the pudding mixture evenly into individual dessert dishes; sprinkle with wafer crumbs. Cover with pie filling; top with remaining pudding mixture. Chill until ready to serve. Garnish with reserved cherries and additional wafer crumbs, if desired. *MAKES 4 to 6 servings*

Prep time: 15 minutes

Black Forest Parfaits

■ Pinwheel Cake and Cream

1 package (4-serving size) JELL-O Instant Pudding and Pie Filling, French Vanilla or Vanilla Flavor
2 cups cold milk
1 cup thawed COOL WHIP Whipped Topping
1 teaspoon grated orange rind
1 small peach or nectarine, cut into bite-size pieces
1 pound cake loaf (about 12 ounces), cut into slices
2 cups summer fruit*

PREPARE pudding mix with milk as directed on package. Let stand 5 minutes or until slightly thickened. Fold in whipped topping, orange rind and peach.

ARRANGE pound cake slices on serving plate. Spoon pudding mixture evenly over center of cake slices. Arrange fruit in pudding mixture. Chill until ready to serve.

MAKES 10 servings

*We suggest any variety of berries, seedless grapes or sliced peaches, nectarines or plums.

Prep time: 15 minutes

■ Trifle Cups

1 package (4-serving size) JELL-O Brand Gelatin, Raspberry Flavor
¾ cup boiling water
1 package BIRDS EYE Quick Thaw Red Raspberries, thawed
Ice cubes
12 shortbread or sugar cookies
1½ cups cold half and half or milk
1 package (4-serving size) JELL-O Instant Pudding and Pie Filling, French Vanilla or Vanilla Flavor
½ cup thawed COOL WHIP Whipped Topping

DISSOLVE gelatin in boiling water. Drain raspberries, reserving syrup. Combine syrup and ice cubes to make 1 cup. Add to gelatin, stirring until ice is melted. Place bowl in larger bowl of ice and water. Let stand, stirring occasionally, until gelatin is slightly thickened, about 5 minutes. Reserve 6 raspberries for garnish, if desired. Stir remaining raspberries into gelatin.

CRUMBLE cookies into individual dessert dishes. Spoon gelatin mixture over cookies; chill until set but not firm.

POUR half and half into small bowl. Add pudding mix. Beat with wire whisk until well blended, about 1 to 2 minutes. Let stand 5 minutes or until slightly thickened. Fold in whipped topping. Spoon over gelatin mixture. Chill until set, about 1 hour. Garnish with reserved raspberries and additional whipped topping, if desired. *MAKES 6 servings*

Prep time: 20 minutes
Chill time: 1 hour

Pinwheel Cake and Cream

Cappucino Cups

12 chocolate wafer cookies
4 teaspoons instant espresso powder*
1 tablespoon hot water
1½ cups cold half and half or milk
1 package (4-serving size) JELL-O Instant Pudding and Pie Filling, French Vanilla or Vanilla Flavor
½ teaspoon ground cinnamon
3½ cups (8 ounces) COOL WHIP Whipped Topping, thawed
1 jar (11.4 ounces) hot fudge sauce
2 to 4 tablespoons coffee liqueur (optional)
Chocolate-covered espresso beans for garnish (optional)

PLACE 1 cookie in each of 12 muffin cups, trimming to fit if necessary.

DISSOLVE espresso powder in hot water in medium bowl. Add half and half, pudding mix and cinnamon. Beat with wire whisk until well blended, 1 to 2 minutes. Let stand 5 minutes or until slightly thickened. Fold in whipped topping. Spoon into muffin cups. Freeze until firm, about 6 hours.

HEAT fudge sauce with liqueur just before serving; keep warm. Run thin knife around rim of each muffin cup; remove dessert. Place on individual dessert plate. (If frozen solid, let stand 5 minutes to soften slightly.)

Top: Cappucino Cups; bottom: Chocolate Orange Cream

SPOON sauce around each dessert. Garnish with additional whipped topping, cinnamon and chocolate-covered espresso beans, if desired.
MAKES 12 servings

*2 tablespoons instant coffee powder may be substituted for the espresso powder.

Prep time: 15 minutes
Freezing time: 6 hours

Chocolate Orange Cream

½ cup cold milk
½ cup cold orange juice
1 to 2 tablespoons orange liqueur or orange juice
1 package (4-serving size) JELL-O Instant Pudding and Pie Filling, Chocolate Flavor
1¾ cups (4 ounces) COOL WHIP Whipped Topping, thawed
5 chocolate dessert cups (optional)
Chocolate-Drizzled Fruit (see page 23 for directions) (optional)

POUR milk, orange juice and liqueur into small bowl. Add pudding mix. Beat with wire whisk until well blended, 1 to 2 minutes. Let stand 2 minutes or until slightly thickened. Fold in whipped topping. Spoon or pipe pudding mixture into chocolate cups or individual dessert glasses. Chill until set, about 1 hour. Garnish with Chocolate-Drizzled Fruit, if desired.
MAKES 4 to 6 servings

Prep time: 10 minutes
Chill time: 1 hour

■ Truffle Treats

6 squares BAKER'S Semi-Sweet
    Chocolate
¼ cup (½ stick) PARKAY Margarine
2⅔ cups (7 ounces) BAKER'S ANGEL
    FLAKE Coconut
1 package (8 ounces)
    PHILADELPHIA BRAND Cream
    Cheese, softened
2½ cups cold half and half or milk
1 package (6-serving size) JELL-O
    Instant Pudding and Pie Filling,
    Chocolate Flavor
2 tablespoons unsweetened cocoa
1 tablespoon confectioners sugar

PLACE chocolate in heavy saucepan
over very low heat; stir constantly until
just melted. Remove 2 tablespoons of
the melted chocolate; set aside.

STIR margarine into remaining
chocolate in saucepan until melted.
Gradually stir in coconut, tossing to
coat evenly. Press mixture into 13×9-
inch baking pan which has been lined
with foil.

BEAT cream cheese at medium speed
of electric mixer until smooth; beat in
reserved 2 tablespoons chocolate.
Gradually mix in half and half. Add
pudding mix. Beat at low speed until
well blended, about 1 minute. Pour
over crust. Freeze until firm, about 4
hours or overnight.

MIX together cocoa and sugar in
small bowl; sift over truffle mixture. Lift
from pan onto cutting board; let stand
10 minutes to soften slightly. Cut into
diamonds, squares or triangles.

MAKES about 20 pieces

Prep time: 15 minutes
Freezing time: 4 hours

■ Quick Chocolate Sauce

¾ cup light corn syrup
1 package (4-serving size) JELL-O
    Instant Pudding and Pie Filling,
    Chocolate or Chocolate Fudge
    Flavor
¾ cup evaporated milk or half and
    half

POUR corn syrup into small bowl. Blend
in pudding mix. Gradually add
evaporated milk, stirring constantly.
Let stand 10 minutes or until slightly
thickened.

SERVE sauce over cake, ice cream or
other desserts.

MAKES about 2 cups

Note: Store leftover sauce in covered
container in refrigerator.

Prep time: 5 minutes

■ Creamy Macaroon Indulgence

1½ cups cold milk
  1 cup (½ pint) sour cream
  2 tablespoons almond liqueur*
  1 package (4-serving size) JELL-O
    Instant Pudding and Pie Filling,
    any flavor
  ½ cup crumbled macaroon cookies

MIX together milk, sour cream and liqueur in small bowl until smooth. Add pudding mix. Beat with wire whisk until well blended, 1 to 2 minutes. Spoon ½ of the pudding mixture into individual dessert dishes.

SPRINKLE crumbled macaroons evenly over pudding. Top with remaining pudding. Chill until ready to serve. Garnish with additional cookies, if desired.   *MAKES 4 servings*

*¼ teaspoon almond extract may be substituted for the almond liqueur.

Prep time: 15 minutes

■ Pear Fans

Canned pear halves, drained
Vanilla Sauce (recipe follows)
Berry Cream Sauce (recipe
follows)
Cinnamon stick, cut into ¾-inch
pieces (optional)
Mint leaves (optional)

SLICE pears lengthwise, cutting almost through stem ends. Place on individual serving plates; spread to form fans (see page 19 for directions). Spoon Vanilla Sauce around pears. Swirl Berry Cream Sauce through Vanilla Sauce to form design (see page 19 for directions). Place cinnamon stick and mint leaf at stem end of each pear, if desired.

Vanilla Sauce

3½ cups cold half and half or milk
1 package (4-serving size) JELL-O
Instant Pudding and Pie Filling,
French Vanilla or Vanilla Flavor

POUR half and half into medium bowl. Add pudding mix. Beat with wire whisk until well blended, 1 to 2 minutes. Let stand 10 minutes or until slightly thickened.   *MAKES 3½ cups*

Berry Cream Sauce

2 packages (10 ounces each)
BIRDS EYE Quick Thaw Red
Raspberries or Strawberries,
thawed
1½ cups cold half and half or milk
1 package (4-serving size) JELL-O
Instant Pudding and Pie Filling,
French Vanilla or Vanilla Flavor

PLACE raspberries in food processor or blender; cover. Process until smooth; strain to remove seeds. Pour half and half into medium bowl. Add pudding mix. Beat with wire whisk until well blended, 1 to 2 minutes. Stir in raspberry puree. Let stand 10 minutes or until slightly thickened.
              MAKES 3½ cups

Note: Store leftover sauces in covered containers in refrigerator.

Prep time: 20 minutes

■ Fruit in Cream

Vanilla Sauce (see Pear Fans, this
page, for recipe)
Assorted fruit*
Quick Chocolate Sauce (see
page 32 for recipe)
Mint leaves (optional)

SPOON Vanilla Sauce onto each serving plate to cover bottom. Arrange fruit in sauce. Swirl Quick Chocolate Sauce through Vanilla Sauce to form design (see page 19 for directions). Garnish with mint leaves, if desired.

*We suggest any variety of berries, mandarin orange sections, melon balls, halved seedless grapes, sliced peaches, kiwifruit or plums.

Prep time: 20 minutes

Top: Pear Fans; bottom: Fruit in Cream

■ Orange Cream Timbales

1 package (4-serving size) JELL-O
   Brand Gelatin, Orange Flavor
1 cup boiling water
½ cup cold water
   Ice cubes
1¾ cups (4 ounces) COOL WHIP
   Whipped Topping, thawed
1 can (11 ounces) mandarin
   orange sections, well drained
   Mint leaves (optional)

DISSOLVE gelatin in boiling water.
Combine cold water and ice cubes to
make 1 cup. Add to gelatin, stirring
until ice is melted. If necessary, place
bowl in larger bowl of ice and water;
let stand, stirring occasionally, until
slightly thickened, about 5 minutes.

FOLD 1⅓ cups of the whipped topping
into gelatin mixture. Pour ½ of the
gelatin mixture evenly into 6 (6-ounce)
custard cups, filling each cup about
halfway. Place dollop of remaining
whipped topping in center of each
dessert; press orange section into
each dollop. Fill cups with remaining
gelatin mixture. Chill until firm, about 3
hours.

PLACE remaining orange sections in
food processor or blender; cover.
Process until smooth. Unmold gelatin
cups onto individual dessert plates.
Spoon orange puree around desserts.
Garnish wth mint leaves, if desired. (Or,
omit orange puree. Garnish desserts
with whole orange sections and mint.)
MAKES 4 servings

Prep time: 20 minutes
Chill time: 3 hours

Orange Cream Timbales

■ Tropical Breeze

1 package (4-serving size) JELL-O
   Brand Gelatin, any flavor
1½ cups boiling tropical blend juice
   drink
1 tablespoon grated lemon,
   orange or lime rind
½ cup cold water
   Ice cubes
¾ cup light corn syrup
2 egg whites, lightly beaten

DISSOLVE gelatin in boiling juice; stir in
rind. Combine cold water and ice
cubes to make 1 cup. Add to gelatin,
stirring until ice is melted. Stir in corn
syrup and egg whites. Place bowl in
larger bowl of ice and water. Let
stand, stirring occasionally, until
gelatin is slightly thickened, about 5
minutes.

BEAT gelatin mixture at high speed of
electric mixer until thick and frothy.
Pour into 9x5-inch loaf pan. Freeze
until firm, about 6 hours or overnight.

SCOOP frozen mixture into individual
dessert glasses. Garnish with Citrus
Curls (see page 18 for directions), if
desired. *MAKES 12 servings*

NOTE: USE ONLY CLEAN EGGS WITH NO
CRACKS IN SHELL.

Prep time: 15 minutes
Freezing time: 6 hours

■ Napoleon Tarts

**1 package (17¼ ounces) frozen
    puff pastry sheets**
1 cup cold milk
1 cup (½ pint) sour cream
**1 package (4-serving size) JELL-O
    Instant Pudding and Pie Filling,
    any flavor**
  **Quick Chocolate Sauce (see
    page 32 for recipe)**

THAW pastry as directed on package. Preheat oven to 375°. Unfold pastry. Cut each sheet into 4 squares. Fold each square in half diagonally. (See Diagram 1.) Cut along 2 unfolded edges, leaving ½-inch rim all around (do not cut completely through to center). (See Diagram 2.) Unfold pastry. Fold outer top righthand corner (A) over to inner bottom lefthand corner (B); fold outer bottom lefthand corner (C) over to inner top righthand corner (D). (See Diagram 3.) Repeat with remaining squares.

PLACE pastries on baking sheets. Pierce bottom of each pastry in several places with fork. Bake for 12 to 15 minutes or until golden. If pastry rises in center, gently press down with fork. Cool on rack.

MIX milk and sour cream in small bowl until smooth. Add pudding mix. Beat with wire whisk until well blended, 1 to 2 minutes. Let stand 5 minutes or until slightly thickened.

SPOON 1 tablespoon Quick Chocolate Sauce onto bottom of each tart shell. Spoon pudding mixture into shells.

DRIZZLE each tart with 1 teaspoon Quick Chocolate Sauce in stripes. Pull wooden pick through stripes in an up and down motion to feather lines. Chill until ready to serve. Serve with remaining sauce.

MAKES 8 servings

Prep time: 20 minutes
Baking time: 12 minutes

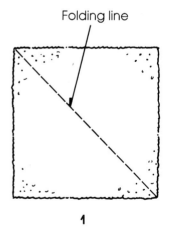

Folding line

1

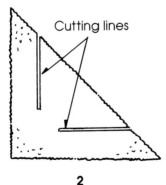

Cutting lines

2

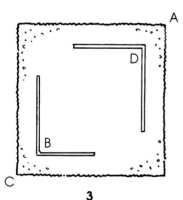

A
D
B
C

3

▪ Pastry Chef Tarts

1 package (10 ounces) pie crust
    mix
1 egg, beaten
1 to 2 tablespoons cold water
1½ cups cold half and half or milk
1 package (4-serving size) JELL-O
    Instant Pudding and Pie Filling,
    French Vanilla or Vanilla Flavor
    Assorted berries or fruit*
    Mint leaves (optional)

PREHEAT oven to 425°. Combine pie
crust mix with egg. Add just enough
water to form dough. Form 2 to 3
tablespoons dough into a round. Press
each round onto bottom and up sides
of each 3- to 4-inch tart pan. (Use tart
pans with removable bottoms, if
possible.) Pierce pastry several times
with fork. Place on baking sheet. Bake
for 10 minutes or until golden. Cool
slightly. Remove tart shells from pans;
cool completely on racks.

POUR half and half into small bowl.
Add pudding mix. Beat with wire whisk
until well blended, 1 to 2 minutes.
Spoon into tart shells. Chill until ready
to serve.

ARRANGE fruit on pudding. Garnish
with mint leaves, if desired.

MAKES 10 servings

*We suggest any variety of berries,
mandarin orange sections, melon
balls, halved seedless grapes, sliced
peaches, kiwifruit or plums.

Note: Individual graham cracker
crumb tart shells may be substituted
for baked tart shells.

Prep time: 20 minutes
Baking time: 10 minutes

▪ Cheesecakes in a Cup

1 package (11 ounces) JELL-O No
    Bake Cheesecake mix
2 tablespoons sugar
⅓ cup PARKAY Margarine, melted
1½ cups cold milk
    Raspberries or sliced strawberries
1 package (4-serving size) JELL-O
    Brand Gelatin, Raspberry or
    Strawberry Flavor
¾ cup boiling water
½ cup cold water
    Ice cubes

COMBINE cheesecake crust crumbs
with sugar in small bowl. Mix in
margarine. Press crumb mixture firmly
onto bottoms of 8 individual dessert
glasses.

MIX milk with cheesecake filling mix at
low speed of electric mixer until
blended. Beat at medium speed 3
minutes. Spoon filling over crusts. Chill
30 minutes. Arrange fruit in single layer
over cheesecake filling.

DISSOLVE gelatin in boiling water.
Combine cold water and ice cubes to
make 1¼ cups. Add to gelatin, stirring
until slightly thickened. Remove any
unmelted ice. Spoon gelatin over fruit.
Chill until firm, about 1½ hours.

MAKES 8 servings

Prep time: 20 minutes
Chill time: 2 hours

Pastry Chef Tarts

■ White Sangria Splash

2 packages (4-serving size each) or
1 package (8-serving size)
JELL-O Brand Gelatin, Lemon
Flavor
1½ cups boiling dry white wine
2½ cups club soda
1 tablespoon lime juice
1 tablespoon orange liqueur or
orange juice
3 cups cut-up fruit*

DISSOLVE gelatin in boiling wine. Stir in club soda, lime juice and liqueur. Place bowl in larger bowl of ice and water. Let stand, stirring occasionally, until gelatin is slightly thickened, about 10 minutes.

FOLD fruit into gelatin mixture. Pour into 6-cup mold. Chill until firm, about 4 hours. Unmold. Garnish with additional fruit, if desired.

MAKES 12 servings

*We suggest strawberry slices, seedless grapes, chopped apples or orange sections.

Prep time: 20 minutes
Chill time: 4 hours

■ Wild Melon Wedges

3 small cantaloupes
1 package (4-serving size) JELL-O
Brand Gelatin, any citrus flavor
1 cup boiling water
½ teaspoon ground ginger
1 can (8 ounces) crushed
pineapple in juice, undrained
Ice cubes
½ cup chopped macadamia nuts or
pecans

CUT melons in half; scoop out seeds. Drain well.

DISSOLVE gelatin in boiling water; stir in ginger. Drain pineapple, reserving juice. Combine juice and ice cubes to make ¾ cup. Add to gelatin, stirring until slightly thickened, about 3 minutes. Remove any unmelted ice.

STIR pineapple and nuts into gelatin mixture. Place melon halves, cut sides up, in small bowls. Spoon gelatin mixture into centers of melons. Chill until firm, about 3 hours. Cut into wedges to serve.

MAKES 12 servings

Prep time: 20 minutes
Chill time: 3 hours

Top: White Sangria Splash; bottom: Wild Melon Wedges

ANYDAY EXTRAS

■ Ambrosia Parfait

1 cup cold milk
1 package (4-serving size) JELL-O
    Instant Pudding and Pie Filling,
    French Vanilla or Vanilla Flavor
1 can (8 ounces) crushed
    pineapple, undrained
1 small banana, chopped
1 cup KRAFT Miniature
    Marshmallows
1 can (11 ounces) mandarin
    orange sections, drained
½ cup sliced almonds, toasted (see
    page 19 for directions)
½ cup BAKER'S ANGEL FLAKE
    Coconut

POUR milk into small bowl. Add
pudding mix. Beat with wire whisk until
well blended, 1 to 2 minutes. Stir in
pineapple, banana and ½ cup of the
marshmallows.

SPOON ⅓ of the pudding mixture into
6 parfait glasses. Add layers of
remaining ingredients, alternating with
layers of pudding. Chill until ready to
serve.   *MAKES 6 servings*

Prep time: 15 minutes

■ Rainbow in a Cloud

1 package (4-serving size) JELL-O
    Brand Gelatin, any flavor
1 cup boiling water
½ cup cold water
1⅓ cups thawed COOL WHIP
    Whipped Topping

DISSOLVE gelatin in boiling water. Add
cold water. Pour into 8-inch square
pan. Chill until firm, at least 3 hours.

DIP pan in warm water about 15
seconds. Cut gelatin into cubes.

DIVIDE whipped topping among 4
dessert glasses, using about ⅓ cup in
each. With back of spoon, make
depression in center; spread topping
up sides of each glass. Spoon gelatin
cubes into glasses. Chill until ready to
serve.   *MAKES 4 servings*

Prep time: 15 minutes
Chill time: 3 hours

Rainbow in a Cloud

■ Ice Cream Shop Pie

1½ cups cold half and half or milk
1 package (4-serving size) JELL-O Instant Pudding and Pie Filling, any flavor
3½ cups (8 ounces) COOL WHIP Whipped Topping, thawed
Ice Cream Shop Ingredients*
1 packaged chocolate, graham cracker or vanilla crumb crust

POUR half and half into large bowl. Add pudding mix. Beat with wire whisk until well blended, 1 to 2 minutes. Let stand 5 minutes or until slightly thickened.

FOLD whipped topping and Ice Cream Shop Ingredients into pudding mixture. Spoon into crust.

FREEZE pie until firm, about 6 hours or overnight. Remove from freezer. Let stand at room temperature about 10 minutes before serving to soften. Store any leftover pie in freezer.
MAKES 8 servings

*Rocky Road Pie: Use any chocolate flavor pudding mix and chocolate crumb crust. Fold in ½ cup *each* BAKER'S Semi-Sweet Real Chocolate Chips, KRAFT Miniature Marshmallows and chopped nuts with whipped topping. Serve with chocolate sauce, if desired.

*Toffee Bar Crunch Pie: Use French vanilla or vanilla flavor pudding mix and graham cracker crumb crust, spreading ⅓ cup butterscotch sauce onto bottom of crust before filling. Fold in 1 cup chopped chocolate-covered English toffee bars (about 6 bars) with whipped topping. Garnish with additional chopped toffee bars, if desired.

*Strawberry Banana Split Pie: Use French vanilla or vanilla flavor pudding mix, reducing half and half to ¾ cup and adding ¾ cup pureed BIRDS EYE Quick Thaw Strawberries with the half and half. Use vanilla crumb crust and line bottom with banana slices. Garnish with whipped topping, maraschino cherries and chopped nuts. Serve with remaining strawberries, pureed, if desired.

*Chocolate Cookie Pie: Use French vanilla or vanilla flavor pudding mix and chocolate crumb crust. Fold in 1 cup chopped chocolate sandwich cookies with whipped topping.

*Nutcracker Pie: Use butter pecan flavor pudding mix and graham cracker crumb crust. Fold in 1 cup chopped mixed nuts with whipped topping.

*Peppermint Stick Pie: Use French vanilla or vanilla flavor pudding mix and chocolate crumb crust. Fold in ½ cup crushed hard peppermint candies, ½ cup BAKER'S Semi-Sweet Real Chocolate Chips and 2 teaspoons peppermint extract with whipped topping.

Prep time: 15 minutes
Freezing time: 6 hours

Top to bottom: Rocky Road Pie; Toffee Bar Crunch Pie; Strawberry Banana Split Pie

■ Creamy Orange Mold

2 packages (4-serving size each) or
    1 package (8-serving size)
    JELL-O Brand Gelatin, Orange
    Flavor
2 cups boiling water
1 pint vanilla ice cream, softened
¾ cup orange juice
    Orange slices (optional)
    Strawberry halves (optional)
    Mint leaves (optional)

DISSOLVE gelatin in boiling water. Spoon in ice cream, stirring until melted and smooth. Stir in orange juice. Pour into 5-cup mold. Chill until firm, about 4 hours. Unmold. Garnish with orange slices, strawberry halves and mint leaves, if desired.

MAKES 10 servings

Prep time: 15 minutes
Chill time: 4 hours

■ Fruit Whip

1 package (4-serving size) JELL-O
    Brand Gelatin, any flavor
1 cup boiling water
½ cup cold water
2 tablespoons lemon juice
    (optional)
2 cups cold milk
1 package (4-serving size) JELL-O
    Instant Pudding and Pie Filling,
    French Vanilla or Vanilla Flavor

DISSOLVE gelatin in boiling water. Add cold water and lemon juice.

POUR milk into small bowl. Add pudding mix. Beat with wire whisk until well blended, 1 to 2 minutes.

PLACE bowl of gelatin in larger bowl of ice and water. Stir until slightly thickened. Beat at high speed of electric mixer until fluffy, thick and doubled in volume. Blend pudding into whipped gelatin. Pour into serving bowl or individual dessert dishes. (Do not mold.) Chill until set, about 2 hours. Garnish as desired.

MAKES 6 to 8 servings

Prep time: 20 minutes
Chill time: 2 hours

Creamy Orange Mold

◼ Layered Fruit Salad

2 packages (4-serving size each) or
   1 package (8-serving size)
   JELL-O Brand Gelatin, Orange or
   Strawberry Flavor
1½ cups boiling water
  1 cup cold water
     Ice cubes
  2 tablespoons lemon juice
  2 cups cut-up fruit*
  1 package (3 ounces)
     PHILADELPHIA BRAND Cream
     Cheese, softened
  ⅛ teaspoon ground cinnamon

DISSOLVE gelatin in boiling water.
Combine cold water and ice cubes to
make 2½ cups. Add to gelatin with
lemon juice; stir until slightly thickened.
Remove any unmelted ice. Set aside 1
cup of the gelatin. Add fruit to
remaining gelatin; pour into serving
bowl.

COMBINE measured gelatin, cream
cheese and cinnamon in blender;
cover. Blend at high speed until
smooth. Spoon carefully over fruited
gelatin. Chill until set, about 2 hours.
Garnish as desired.

MAKES 10 servings

*We suggest sliced bananas,
strawberries, halved seedless grapes
or orange segments.

Prep time: 20 minutes
Chill time: 2 hours

◼ Peach Melba Dessert

1 package (4-serving size) JELL-O
   Brand Gelatin, Peach Flavor
2 cups boiling water
¾ cup cold water
1 package (4-serving size) JELL-O
   Brand Gelatin, Raspberry Flavor
1 pint vanilla ice cream, softened
1 can (8¾ ounces) sliced peaches,
   drained*
½ cup fresh raspberries
   Mint leaves (optional)

DISSOLVE peach flavor gelatin in 1 cup
of the boiling water. Add cold water.
Chill until slightly thickened.

DISSOLVE raspberry flavor gelatin in
remaining 1 cup boiling water. Spoon
in ice cream, stirring until melted and
smooth. Pour into serving bowl. Chill
until set but not firm.

ARRANGE peach slices and
raspberries on ice cream mixture in
bowl. Add mint leaves, if desired.
Spoon peach gelatin over fruit. Chill
until firm, about 3 hours.

MAKES 10 servings

*1 fresh peach, peeled and sliced,
may be substituted for canned
peaches.

Prep time: 20 minutes
Chill time: 4 hours

Peach Melba Dessert

■ Creamy Italian Cheesecake

⅓ cup chopped dried apricots
1 to 2 tablespoons rum
1 package (11 ounces) JELL-O No Bake Cheesecake mix
1 cup cold milk
¾ cup ricotta cheese
¼ cup slivered or sliced almonds, toasted (see page 19 for directions)
¼ cup BAKER'S Semi-Sweet Real Chocolate Chips, coarsely chopped
1½ teaspoons grated lemon rind

SOAK apricots in rum in small bowl; set aside.

PREPARE crumb crust as directed on cheesecake package.

MIX together milk and cheese in small bowl until smooth. Add cheesecake filling mix. Beat at medium speed of electric mixer 3 minutes or until very thick. Fold in apricots with rum, almonds, chocolate chips and lemon rind. Spoon filling mixture into crust. Chill until firm, at least 1 hour. Garnish with additional almonds, apricots and chocolate chips, if desired.

MAKES 8 servings

Prep time: 20 minutes
Chill time: 1 hour

■ Triple Layer Desserts

3 cups cold half and half
3 cups cold milk
¼ cup chocolate liqueur (optional)
1 package (4-serving size) JELL-O Instant Pudding and Pie Filling, French Vanilla or Vanilla Flavor
2 packages (4-serving size each) JELL-O Instant Pudding and Pie Filling, Chocolate Flavor
½ cup thawed COOL WHIP Whipped Topping
2 squares BAKER'S Semi-Sweet Chocolate, melted
Chocolate Cutouts (see page 23 for directions) (optional)

POUR 1 cup of the half and half, 1 cup of the milk and 2 tablespoons of the liqueur into small bowl. Add vanilla pudding mix. Beat with wire whisk until well blended, 1 to 2 minutes. Let stand until slightly thickened, about 5 minutes. Spoon into individual dessert glasses.

POUR remaining 2 cups half and half and 2 cups milk into medium bowl. Add chocolate pudding mix. Beat with wire whisk until well blended, 1 to 2 minutes. Fold whipped topping into ½ of the chocolate pudding; let stand until slightly thickened. Spoon over vanilla pudding in glasses. Stir melted chocolate and remaining 2 tablespoons liqueur into remaining chocolate pudding; let stand until slightly thickened. Spoon into glasses. Chill until ready to serve. Garnish with Chocolate Cutouts, if desired.

MAKES 8 servings

Prep time: 20 minutes

Triple Layer Desserts

■ Cherry-Topped Easier Than Pie

14 whole graham crackers
2 cups cold milk
1 package (6-serving size) JELL-O Instant Pudding and Pie Filling, French Vanilla or Vanilla Flavor
1 cup thawed COOL WHIP Whipped Topping
1 can (21 ounces) cherry pie filling

ARRANGE ⅓ of the crackers on bottom of 9-inch square pan, cutting crackers to fit, if necessary.

POUR milk into small bowl. Add pudding mix. Beat with wire whisk until well blended, 1 to 2 minutes. Let stand 5 minutes. Fold in whipped topping.

SPREAD ½ of the pudding mixture over crackers. Add second layer of crackers; top with remaining pudding mixture and remaining crackers. Chill 3 hours.

CUT dessert into squares. Spoon pie filling over each square. Garnish with additional whipped topping, if desired.   *MAKES 8 to 10 servings*

Prep time: 15 minutes
Chill time: 3 hours

■ Sour Cream Pudding

1 package (4-serving size) JELL-O
    Pudding and Pie Filling, any
    flavor except lemon
3 tablespoons sugar
1 cup water
1 cup (½ pint) sour cream

STIR pudding mix and sugar into water in 1½-quart microwavable bowl; blend well. Microwave on HIGH 6 minutes, stirring every 2 minutes, until mixture comes to boil. Stir well. Cool 5 minutes, stirring twice.

STIR in sour cream until well blended. Pour into serving bowl or individual dessert dishes. Chill until ready to serve. Garnish as desired.

MAKES 4 servings

Note: Ovens vary; cooking time is approximate.

Range-Top Preparation: Stir pudding mix and sugar into water in medium saucepan; blend well. Cook and stir over medium heat until mixture comes to full boil. Cool 5 minutes, stirring twice. Stir in sour cream until well blended. Pour into serving bowl or individual dessert dishes. Chill until ready to serve.

Prep time: 10 minutes

■ Blender Cheese Pie

1 package (4-serving size) JELL-O
    Brand Gelatin, any flavor
1 cup boiling water
1 package (3 ounces)
    PHILADELPHIA BRAND Cream
    Cheese, cubed
½ cup cold water
    Ice cubes
1¾ cups (4 ounces) COOL WHIP
    Whipped Topping, thawed
1 packaged graham cracker
    crumb crust

COMBINE gelatin and boiling water in blender; cover. Blend at low speed until gelatin is dissolved, about 1 minute. Add cream cheese. Blend at low speed 30 seconds. Combine cold water and ice cubes to make 1 cup. Add to gelatin mixture in blender; stir until ice is partially melted.

ADD whipped topping to gelatin mixture. Blend at high speed until ice is melted, about 30 seconds. Pour into crust. Chill 2 hours. Garnish as desired.

MAKES 8 servings

Prep time: 20 minutes
Chill time: 2 hours

■ Pudding Parfait

1 package (4-serving size) JELL-O Brand Gelatin, any flavor
¾ cup boiling water
½ cup cold water
Ice cubes
2 cups cold milk
1 package (4-serving size) JELL-O Instant Pudding and Pie Filling, any flavor

DISSOLVE gelatin in boiling water. Combine cold water and ice cubes to make 1¼ cups. Add to gelatin, stirring until slightly thickened. Remove any unmelted ice.

POUR milk into small bowl. Add pudding mix. Beat with wire whisk until well blended, 1 to 2 minutes. Alternately spoon pudding and gelatin into individual dessert dishes. Chill 1 hour. Garnish as desired.

MAKES 8 servings

Prep time: 15 minutes
Chill time: 1 hour

■ Fruit Delight

1 package (4-serving size) JELL-O Brand Gelatin, any flavor
¾ cup boiling water
½ cup cold water
Ice cubes
1 cup fresh or canned fruit (optional)

COMBINE gelatin and boiling water in blender container; cover. Blend at low speed until gelatin is dissolved, about 1 minute. Combine cold water and ice cubes to make 1 cup. Add to gelatin in blender. Stir until ice is partially melted; blend at high speed 30 seconds.

POUR gelatin into individual dessert glasses or serving bowl. Spoon in fruit. Chill until firm, about 20 minutes. (Dessert layers as it chills and will have a clear layer topped with a frothy layer.) Garnish as desired.

MAKES 6 servings

Note: If desired when using canned fruit, ½ cup drained juice or syrup may be substituted for ½ cup cold water.

Prep time: 10 minutes
Chill time: 20 minutes

■ Banana Orange Mold

2 packages (4-serving size each) or
    1 package (8-serving size)
    JELL-O Brand Gelatin, Orange
    Flavor
2 cups boiling water
¾ cup cold ginger ale
1 can (11 ounces) mandarin
    orange sections, drained
1 medium banana, chopped
    (about ¾ cup)
½ cup MIRACLE WHIP Salad Dressing
1 cup thawed COOL WHIP Whipped
    Topping

DISSOLVE gelatin in boiling water. Measure 1¼ cups gelatin into small bowl; set aside. Add ginger ale to remaining gelatin. Chill until thickened; fold in orange sections and banana. Pour into 5-cup mold. Chill until set but not firm.

WHISK reserved gelatin gradually into salad dressing. Fold in whipped topping; pour over gelatin in mold. Chill until firm, about 4 hours. Unmold. Serve on crisp salad greens, if desired.
MAKES 10 servings

Prep time: 20 minutes
Chill time: 4 hours

■ Fresh Fruit Dessert

1½ cups fresh fruit*
2 tablespoons sugar*
1 package (4-serving size) JELL-O
    Brand Gelatin, any flavor
1 cup boiling water
1½ cups cold water*

COMBINE fruit and sugar; let stand 10 minutes. Dissolve gelatin in boiling water. Add cold water. Chill until thickened.

STIR fruit mixture into gelatin. Chill 1 hour. (Dessert will be soft-set, not firm.)

SPOON gelatin mixture into individual dessert glasses or serving bowl. Garnish with thawed whipped topping, if desired.
MAKES 8 servings

*Canned or thawed frozen fruit may be substituted for fresh fruit. Omit sugar. Drain syrup from fruit; add cold water to syrup to make 1½ cups.

Prep time: 15 minutes
Chill time: 1½ hours

Any Season Light and Fruity Pie

1 package (4-serving size) JELL-O Brand Gelatin, any flavor
⅔ cup boiling water
½ cup cold water
Ice cubes
3½ cups (8 ounces) COOL WHIP Whipped Topping, thawed
Any Season Ingredients*
1 packaged graham cracker crumb crust

DISSOLVE gelatin in boiling water. Combine cold water and ice cubes to make 1¼ cups. Add to gelatin, stirring until slightly thickened. Remove any unmelted ice.

BLEND whipped topping into gelatin, using wire whisk. Fold in Any Season Ingredients. Chill until mixture is very thick.

SPOON gelatin mixture into crust. Chill 2 hours. Garnish with additional fruit and whipped topping, if desired.
MAKES 8 servings

*Citrus Snowflake Pie (winter): Use orange flavor gelatin. Fold in 1 cup drained mandarin orange sections, 1 small banana, sliced, and 2 tablespoons orange liqueur (optional). Garnish with additional whipped topping, mandarin orange sections and Toasted Coconut (see page 21 for directions), if desired.

*Any Berry Pie (spring): Use raspberry or strawberry flavor gelatin. Fold in ½ cup each blueberries, raspberries and sliced strawberries and 2

Citrus Snowflake Pie

tablespoons raspberry liqueur (optional). Garnish with additional whipped topping and berries, if desired.

*Creamy Daiquiri Pie (summer): Use lime flavor gelatin. Add ½ teaspoon grated lime rind, 2 tablespoons lime juice and 3 tablespoons rum (optional). Garnish with additional whipped topping and Citrus Curls (see page 18 for directions), if desired.

*Autumn Harvest Pie (fall): Use lemon flavor gelatin. Fold in 1 ripe pear, chopped, and 1 tablespoon lemon juice. Garnish with additional whipped topping and lemon slices, if desired.

Prep time: 20 minutes
Chill time: 2 hours

Lemon Mousse

1 cup cold milk
1 package (4-serving size) JELL-O Instant Pudding and Pie Filling, Lemon Flavor
1¾ cups (4 ounces) COOL WHIP Whipped Topping, thawed
Raspberry Sauce (see page 67 for recipe) (optional)

POUR milk into small bowl. Add pudding mix. Beat with wire whisk until well blended, 1 to 2 minutes.

FOLD whipped topping into pudding. Pour into serving bowl or individual dessert dishes. Chill until ready to serve. Serve with Raspberry Sauce, if desired. *MAKES 4 to 6 servings*

Prep time: 10 minutes

■ Basic Bavarian

1 package (4-serving size) JELL-O Brand Gelatin, any flavor
1 cup boiling water
1 cup cold water
1¾ cups (4 ounces) COOL WHIP Whipped Topping, thawed

DISSOLVE gelatin in boiling water. Add cold water. Chill until slightly thickened. Fold in 1½ cups of the whipped topping.

POUR gelatin mixture into 4-cup mold or individual molds. Chill until firm, at least 4 hours. Unmold. Garnish with remaining whipped topping and fruit, if desired. *MAKES 6 servings*

Fruit Juice Bavarian: Substitute 1 cup cold fruit juice for cold water.

Two Flavor Bavarian: Prepare dessert twice, using 2 different gelatin flavors. Layer gelatins in parfait glasses. Makes 12 servings.

Fruited Bavarian: Add 1 cup sliced fresh fruit (except pineapple, kiwifruit, mango, papaya or figs) after folding in whipped topping.

Prep time: 15 minutes
Chill time: 4 hours

■ Boston Cream Parfaits

1 package (4-serving size) JELL-O Instant Pudding and Pie Filling, French Vanilla or Vanilla Flavor
2 cups cold milk
½ cup (about) chocolate syrup
1 cup thawed COOL WHIP Whipped Topping

PREPARE pudding mix with milk as directed on package. Pour ½ of the pudding into 6 parfait glasses. Top with ½ of the chocolate syrup and the whipped topping. Repeat with remaining pudding and chocolate syrup. Chill until ready to serve. Garnish with additional whipped topping, if desired.
MAKES 6 servings

Prep time: 20 minutes

■ Cranberry-Apple Dessert

1 package (4-serving size) JELL-O Brand Gelatin, Blackberry Flavor
1 cup boiling water
¾ cup cranberry juice
1 cup diced apples
¼ cup chopped nuts

DISSOLVE gelatin in boiling water. Add cranberry juice. Chill until slightly thickened. Fold in apples and nuts.

SPOON gelatin mixture into 3-cup mold, individual molds or dessert glasses. Chill until firm, about 2 hours. Unmold. Garnish as desired.
MAKES 4 to 6 servings

Prep time: 10 minutes
Chill time: 2 hours

■ Banana Split Dessert

1 package (4-serving size) JELL-O
    Brand Gelatin, any flavor
¾ cup boiling water
1 cup vanilla ice cream, softened
½ cup crushed ice
    COOL WHIP Whipped Topping,
      thawed
    Sliced bananas
    Strawberry halves
    Pineapple chunks
    Chopped nuts

COMBINE gelatin and boiling water in blender; cover. Blend at low speed until gelatin is dissolved, about 1 minute. Add ice cream and crushed ice. Blend at high speed until ice is melted, about 30 seconds.

POUR gelatin mixture into serving bowl. Chill 20 minutes. Top with whipped topping, fruit and nuts.

MAKES 4 servings

Prep time: 10 minutes
Chill time: 20 minutes

■ Pudding Cookie Surprise

1 package (4-serving size) JELL-O
  Pudding and Pie Filling, any
  flavor
2 cups milk
6 gingersnap cookies, crumbled
⅓ cup chopped nuts
2 tablespoons PARKAY Margarine,
  melted

STIR pudding mix into milk in 1½-quart microwavable bowl. Microwave on HIGH 6 minutes, stirring every 2 minutes, until mixture comes to boil. Stir well. Place plastic wrap on surface of pudding. Chill 2 hours.

MIX cookie crumbs, nuts and margarine in small bowl. Place about 2 tablespoons crumb mixture in each of 4 dessert glasses. Stir pudding; spoon into glasses. Sprinkle with remaining crumb mixture.

MAKES 4 servings

Note: Ovens vary; cooking time is approximate.

Range-Top Preparation: Stir pudding mix into milk in medium saucepan. Cook and stir over medium heat until mixture comes to full boil. Place plastic wrap on surface of pudding. Chill 2 hours. Continue as directed above.

Prep time: 20 minutes
Chill time: 2 hours

■ Warm Apple-Walnut Pudding

1 package (4-serving size) JELL-O
  Pudding and Pie Filling,
  Butterscotch Flavor
1¾ cups milk
2 medium apples, peeled and
  thinly sliced
½ cup chopped walnuts
½ teaspoon ground cinnamon

STIR pudding mix into milk in 2-quart microwavable bowl. Stir in apples, walnuts and cinnamon. Microwave on HIGH 3 minutes; stir well. Microwave 2 minutes longer or until mixture comes to boil; stir. Cool slightly. Serve warm topped with vanilla ice cream, if desired. *MAKES 4 servings*

Note: Ovens vary; cooking time is approximate.

Prep time: 15 minutes

Circa 1915

HOLIDAYS AND MORE

■ Eggnog Cheesecake

2 packages (5½ ounces each)
　　chocolate-laced pirouette
　　cookies
⅓ cup graham cracker crumbs
3 tablespoons PARKAY Margarine,
　　melted
2 packages (8 ounces each)
　　PHILADELPHIA BRAND Cream
　　Cheese, softened
2 cups cold prepared eggnog
2 cups cold milk
2 packages (4-serving size each)
　　JELL-O Instant Pudding and Pie
　　Filling, French Vanilla or Vanilla
　　Flavor
1 tablespoon rum
⅛ teaspoon ground nutmeg
　　COOL WHIP Whipped Topping,
　　thawed (optional)
　　Ribbon (optional)

RESERVE 1 cookie for garnish, if
desired. Cut 1-inch piece off one end
of each of the remaining cookies.
Crush 1-inch pieces into crumbs; set
aside remaining cookies for sides of
cake. Combine cookie crumbs,
graham cracker crumbs and
margarine until well mixed. Press
crumb mixture firmly onto bottom of
9-inch springform pan.

BEAT cream cheese at low speed of
electric mixer until smooth. Gradually
add 1 cup of the eggnog, blending
until mixture is very smooth. Add
remaining eggnog, milk, pudding mix,
rum and nutmeg. Beat until well
blended, about 1 minute. Pour cream
cheese mixture carefully into pan. Chill
until firm, about 3 hours. Run hot metal
spatula or knife around edges of pan
before removing sides of pan.

PRESS remaining cookies, cut sides
down, into sides of cake. Garnish with
whipped topping and reserved
cookie, if desired. Tie ribbon around
cake, if desired.

MAKES 12 servings

Prep time: 45 minutes
Chill time: 3 hours

*Top to bottom: Eggnog Cheesecake;
Holiday Fruitcake and Marzipan Fruits
(page 66); Raspberry Gift Box (page 67)*

■ Holiday Fruitcake

1 cup chopped candied fruit
⅔ cup pitted dates, chopped
½ cup chopped walnuts
¼ cup brandy or orange juice
1 package (6-serving size) JELL-O
   Instant Pudding and Pie Filling,
   Vanilla Flavor
1 package (2-layer size) yellow
   cake mix
4 eggs
1 cup (½ pint) sour cream
⅓ cup vegetable oil
1 tablespoon grated orange rind
⅔ cup cold milk
   Marzipan Fruits (recipe follows)
   (optional)

MIX together candied fruit, dates, walnuts and brandy.

RESERVE ⅓ cup pudding mix; set aside. Combine cake mix, remaining pudding mix, eggs, sour cream, oil and orange rind in large bowl. Beat at low speed of electric mixer just to moisten, scraping sides of bowl often. Beat at medium speed 4 minutes. Stir in fruit mixture.

POUR batter into well-greased and floured 10-inch fluted tube pan. Bake at 350° for 45 minutes or until cake tester inserted in center comes out clean. Cool in pan 15 minutes. Remove from pan; finish cooling on wire rack.

BEAT reserved pudding mix and milk in small bowl until smooth. Spoon over top of cake to glaze. Garnish with Marzipan Fruits, if desired.

MAKES 12 servings

Prep time: 30 minutes
Baking time: 45 minutes

■ Marzipan Fruits

1¾ cups BAKER'S ANGEL FLAKE
   Coconut, finely chopped
1 package (4-serving size) JELL-O
   Brand Gelatin, any flavor
1 cup ground blanched almonds
⅔ cup sweetened condensed milk
1½ teaspoons sugar
1 teaspoon almond extract
   Food coloring (optional)
   Whole cloves (optional)
   Citron or angelica (optional)

MIX together coconut, gelatin, almonds, milk, sugar and extract. Shape by hand into small fruits, or use small candy molds. If desired, use food coloring to paint details on fruit; add whole cloves and citron for stems and blossom ends. Chill until dry. Store in covered container at room temperature up to 1 week.

MAKES 2 to 3 dozen confections

Prep time: 30 minutes

■ Raspberry Gift Box

**2 packages (4-serving size each) or
1 package (8-serving size)
JELL-O Brand Gelatin, Raspberry
Flavor
1½ cups boiling water
¾ cup cran-raspberry juice
Ice cubes
3½ cups (8 ounces) COOL WHIP
Whipped Topping, thawed
Raspberry Sauce (recipe follows)
Gumdrop Ribbon (see page 20 for
directions) (optional)
Frosted Cranberries (see page 18
for directions) (optional)**

DISSOLVE gelatin in boiling water.
Combine cran-raspberry juice and ice
cubes to make 1¾ cups. Add to
gelatin, stirring until ice is melted. Chill
until slightly thickened. Fold in
whipped topping. Pour into 9×5-inch
loaf pan. Chill until firm, about 4 hours.

PREPARE Raspberry Sauce, Gumdrop
Ribbon and Frosted Cranberries, if
desired.

UNMOLD gelatin mixture onto serving
plate. Cut Gumdrop Ribbon into 2
(10×1-inch) strips and 1 (5×1-inch)
strip. Place strips on raspberry loaf,
piecing strips together as necessary,
to resemble ribbon. Cut 7 (3×1-inch)
strips; form into bow. Place on
gumdrop ribbon. Decorate with
Frosted Cranberries. Serve with
Raspberry Sauce.

MAKES 8 servings

Raspberry Sauce

**2 packages (10 ounces each)
BIRDS EYE Quick Thaw Red
Raspberries, thawed
2 teaspoons cornstarch**

PLACE raspberries in food processor or
blender; cover. Process until smooth;
strain to remove seeds. Combine
cornstarch with small amount of the
raspberries in medium saucepan; add
remaining raspberries. Bring to boil
over medium heat, stirring constantly;
boil 1 minute. Chill.   *MAKES 2 cups*

Prep time: 30 minutes
Chill time: 4 hours

■ Brandied Cherry Ring

**1 can (16 ounces) pitted dark sweet
cherries, undrained
⅓ cup brandy
2 packages (4-serving size each) or
1 package (8-serving size)
JELL-O Brand Gelatin, Cherry or
Black Cherry Flavor
2 cups boiling water
1¾ cups (4 ounces) COOL WHIP
Whipped Topping, thawed**

DRAIN cherries, measuring syrup. Add
cold water to syrup to make 1 cup.
Cut cherries in half. Heat brandy; pour
over cherries. Let stand 30 minutes;
drain, reserving brandy.

DISSOLVE gelatin in boiling water. Add
measured liquid and brandy. Chill until
thickened. Add cherries to ½ of the
gelatin. Pour into 5-cup ring mold. Chill
until set but not firm.

FOLD 1 cup of the whipped topping
into remaining gelatin. Spoon into
mold. Chill until firm, about 4 hours.
Unmold. Garnish with remaining
whipped topping.

MAKES 10 servings

Prep time: 30 minutes
Chill time: 4 hours

■ Christmas Tree Poke Cake

2 packages (2-layer size each) white cake mix
1 package (4-serving size) JELL-O Brand Gelatin, Strawberry Flavor
1 package (4-serving size) JELL-O Brand Gelatin, Lime Flavor
2 cups boiling water
2⅔ cups (7 ounces) BAKER'S ANGEL FLAKE Coconut
Green food coloring
5¼ cups (12 ounces) COOL WHIP Whipped Topping, thawed
Assorted gumdrops (optional)
Peppermint candies (optional)
Red string licorice (optional)

PREPARE 1 cake mix as directed on package. Pour batter into greased and floured 9-inch square pan. Bake at 325° for 50 to 55 minutes or until cake tester inserted in center comes out clean. Cool 10 minutes. Remove from pan; finish cooling on rack. Repeat with remaining cake mix.

PLACE cake layers, top sides up, in 2 clean 9-inch square pans. Pierce cakes with large fork at ½-inch intervals.

DISSOLVE each flavor of gelatin in separate bowl, using 1 cup of the boiling water for each. Carefully pour strawberry flavor gelatin over 1 cake layer and lime flavor gelatin over second cake layer. Chill 3 hours.

TOAST ⅓ cup of the coconut (see page 21 for directions); set aside. Tint remaining coconut with green food coloring (see page 21 for directions).

DIP 1 cake pan in warm water 10 seconds; unmold. Place right side up on large serving plate or cutting board. Cut cake as shown in Diagram 1. Arrange pieces in Christmas tree shape (Diagram 2), using small amount of whipped topping to hold pieces together. Top with about 1½ cups of the whipped topping. Unmold second cake layer; cut into pieces as shown in Diagram 1. Place pieces on first layer, using small amount of whipped topping to hold pieces together. Use remaining whipped topping to frost entire cake.

SPRINKLE trunk of tree with toasted coconut. Sprinkle remaining cake with green coconut. Decorate with gumdrops, peppermint candies and licorice, if desired. Chill until ready to serve.   *MAKES 24 servings*

Prep time: 30 minutes
Chill time: 3 hours

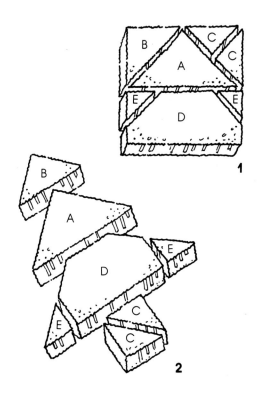

■ Christmas Ribbon

**2 packages (4-serving size each) or
1 package (8-serving size)
JELL-O Brand Gelatin,
Strawberry Flavor**
5 cups boiling water
**⅔ cup sour cream or plain or vanilla
yogurt**
**2 packages (4-serving size each) or
1 package (8-serving size)
JELL-O Brand Gelatin, Lime
Flavor**

DISSOLVE strawberry gelatin in 2½
cups of the boiling water. Pour 1½
cups gelatin into 6-cup ring mold. Chill
until set but not firm, about 30 minutes.
Chill remaining gelatin in bowl until
slightly thickened; gradually blend in
⅓ cup of the sour cream. Spoon over
gelatin in mold. Chill until set but not
firm, about 15 minutes.

REPEAT with lime gelatin, remaining 2½
cups boiling water and ⅓ cup sour
cream, chilling dissolved gelatin
before measuring and pouring into
mold. Chill at least 2 hours. Unmold.
MAKES 12 servings

Prep time: 30 minutes
Chill time: 3 hours

■ Gaiety Pastel Cookies

1½ cups (3 sticks) PARKAY Margarine
1 cup sugar
**1 package (4-serving size) JELL-O
Brand Gelatin, any flavor***
1 egg
1 teaspoon vanilla
3½ cups all-purpose flour
**1 teaspoon CALUMET Baking
Powder**
**Additional JELL-O Brand Gelatin,
any flavor***

BEAT margarine at medium speed of
electric mixer until light and fluffy.
Gradually beat in sugar and 1
package of the gelatin. Mix in egg
and vanilla. Stir in flour and baking
powder until well blended.

FORCE dough through cookie press
onto greased baking sheets. Sprinkle
with additional gelatin. Decorate, if
desired. Bake at 400° for 13 minutes for
medium cookies (about 2-inch
diameter) or 8 minutes for small
cookies (about 1-inch diameter) or
until golden brown around edges.
Remove; cool on racks. Store in loosely
covered container.
*MAKES about 5 dozen medium
cookies or 10 dozen small cookies*

*For best results, use same flavor
gelatin to flavor cookies and for
garnish.

Prep time: 40 minutes
Baking time: 40 minutes

Christmas Ribbon

■ Ginger Bears

1½ cups all-purpose flour
1½ teaspoons ground ginger
1 teaspoon ground cinnamon
½ teaspoon baking soda
½ cup (1 stick) PARKAY Margarine
½ cup firmly packed brown sugar
1 package (4-serving size) JELL-O Pudding and Pie Filling, Butterscotch Flavor
1 egg
Confectioners Sugar Glaze (recipe follows) or 1 tube prepared decorating icing
Ribbon (optional)

MIX together flour, spices and baking soda. Beat margarine at low speed of electric mixer until light and fluffy; beat in sugar, pudding mix and egg. Gradually add flour mixture, beating until smooth after each addition. Chill dough until firm enough to handle.

ROLL out dough to ⅛-inch thickness on floured surface; cut with 3-inch floured teddy bear cookie cutter. Place on greased baking sheets. Bake at 350° for 10 minutes or until lightly browned. Remove; cool on rack. Decorate cooled cookies with Confectioners Sugar Glaze or icing. Attach ribbon bow ties, if desired.
MAKES about 2½ dozen cookies

Confectioners Sugar Glaze

2½ cups confectioners sugar
3 tablespoons (about) hot milk or water

PLACE sugar in small bowl. Gradually add milk, blending well.
MAKES 1⅓ cups

Prep time: 30 minutes
Baking time: 30 minutes

■ Christmas Popcorn Teddy Bear

18 cups popped popcorn
1 cup light corn syrup
½ cup sugar
1 package (4-serving size) JELL-O Brand Gelatin, Strawberry or Lime Flavor
Jelly beans or gumdrops (optional)
Ribbon (optional)

PLACE popcorn in large greased bowl. Combine corn syrup and sugar in medium saucepan. Bring to full rolling boil, stirring constantly; boil 1 minute. Remove from heat. Stir in gelatin until dissolved. Pour over popcorn; toss to coat well. Cool 5 minutes.

FORM about ⅔ of the popcorn mixture into 2 balls, one larger than the other, forming bear's body and head. Shape remaining popcorn into arms, legs and ears; attach to body and head. Use jelly beans or gumdrops for eyes and nose. Attach ribbon bow tie, if desired.
MAKES 1 large teddy bear

Popcorn Balls: Prepare popcorn mixture as directed; shape into 2-inch balls. Makes about 2 dozen popcorn balls.

Note: For ease in handling, grease hands slightly before shaping popcorn mixture into desired shapes.

Prep time: 20 minutes

Top: Christmas Popcorn Teddy Bear; bottom: Ginger Bears

■ Spiced Cranberry-Orange Mold

1 bag (12 ounces) cranberries*
½ cup sugar*
2 packages (4-serving size each) or
   1 package (8-serving size)
   JELL-O Brand Gelatin, Orange or
   Lemon Flavor
1½ cups boiling water
1 cup cold water*
1 tablespoon lemon juice
¼ teaspoon ground cinnamon
⅛ teaspoon ground cloves
1 orange, sectioned and diced
½ cup chopped walnuts
   Orange slices (optional)
   White kale or curly leaf lettuce
   (optional)

PLACE cranberries in food processor; cover. Process until finely chopped. Mix with sugar; set aside.

DISSOLVE gelatin in boiling water. Add cold water, lemon juice and spices. Chill until thickened. Fold in cranberry mixture, oranges and walnuts. Spoon into 5-cup mold. Chill until firm, about 4 hours. Unmold. Garnish with orange slices and kale, if desired.

MAKES 10 servings

*1 can (16 ounces) whole berry cranberry sauce may be substituted for fresh cranberries. Omit sugar and reduce cold water to ½ cup.

Prep time: 20 minutes
Chill time: 4 hours

■ Holiday Fruit and Nut Mold

2 packages (4-serving size each) or
   1 package (8-serving size)
   JELL-O Brand Gelatin, any flavor
2 cups boiling water
1¼ cups ginger ale or lemon-lime
   carbonated beverage
⅛ teaspoon ground cinnamon
⅛ teaspoon ground cloves
⅛ teaspoon ground nutmeg
½ cup chopped mixed dried fruit
⅓ cup currants or raisins
⅓ cup chopped candied or
   maraschino cherries
⅓ cup chopped pecans or walnuts

DISSOLVE gelatin in boiling water. Add ginger ale and spices. Chill until slightly thickened. Fold in fruit and nuts. Spoon into 5-cup mold or 9×5-inch loaf pan. Chill until firm, about 4 hours. Unmold. Serve with whipped topping, if desired.   *MAKES 10 servings*

Prep time: 20 minutes
Chill time: 4 hours

Spiced Cranberry-Orange Mold

■ Pudding Pecan Pie

1 cup light or dark corn syrup
1 package (4-serving size) JELL-O
    Instant Pudding and Pie Filling,
    Butterscotch, French Vanilla or
    Vanilla Flavor
¾ cup evaporated milk
1 egg, slightly beaten
1 cup chopped pecans
1 unbaked 8-inch pie shell
    COOL WHIP Whipped Topping,
    thawed (optional)

POUR corn syrup into medium bowl.
Blend in pie filling mix. Gradually add
evaporated milk and egg, stirring until
well blended. Add pecans. Pour into
pie shell.

BAKE pie at 375° for 45 minutes or until
top is firm and just begins to crack.
Cool at least 3 hours before cutting to
serve. Garnish with whipped topping
and additional pecans, if desired.

MAKES 8 servings

Prep time: 15 minutes
Baking time: 45 minutes

■ Spiced Peach Mold

1 can (16 ounces) sliced peaches,
    undrained
2 packages (4-serving size each) or
    1 package (8-serving size)
    JELL-O Brand Gelatin, Orange
    Flavor
½ teaspoon ground cinnamon
⅛ teaspoon ground cloves
2 cups boiling water
3 tablespoons vinegar
    Yogurt Sauce (recipe follows)
    (optional)

DRAIN peaches, reserving syrup. Add
water to syrup to make 1¼ cups. Dice
peaches; set aside.

COMBINE gelatin and spices in
medium bowl. Add boiling water; stir
until gelatin is dissolved. Add
measured liquid and vinegar. Chill until
thickened. Stir in peaches. Pour into
5-cup mold. Chill until firm, about 4
hours. Unmold. Cut into slices; serve
with Yogurt Sauce, if desired.

MAKES 10 servings

Yogurt Sauce

1 container (8 ounces) vanilla
    yogurt
1 tablespoon orange juice
⅛ teaspoon ground cinnamon

MIX together all ingredients until well
blended. Chill until ready to serve.

MAKES 1 cup

Prep time: 20 minutes
Chill time: 4 hours

■ Chocolate-Apricot Steamed Pudding

½ cup dried apricots, finely chopped
¼ cup apricot brandy or fruit juice
2 packages (4-serving size each) JELL-O Pudding and Pie Filling, Chocolate Flavor
¼ cup all-purpose flour
¼ teaspoon CALUMET Baking Powder
¼ teaspoon salt
4 egg whites
¼ cup sugar
4 egg yolks
¼ cup (½ stick) PARKAY Margarine, melted
½ teaspoon vanilla
1 package (4-serving size) JELL-O Pudding and Pie Filling, Vanilla Flavor
3 cups milk

SOAK apricots in 2 tablespoons of the brandy; set aside.

COMBINE chocolate pudding mix, flour, baking powder and salt; set aside. Beat egg whites at high speed of electric mixer until foamy. Gradually add sugar; continue beating until stiff peaks form. Beat egg yolks in large bowl until thick and light in color. Fold in egg whites. Gently stir in dry ingredients. Fold in apricot mixture, margarine and vanilla.

POUR chocolate pudding mixture into well-greased 1-quart mold; cover tightly with foil. Set mold on rack in large saucepot. Add enough hot water to saucepot to come halfway up side of mold. Heat water to boiling. Reduce heat; cover and steam 1½ hours.

COMBINE vanilla pudding mix with milk in medium saucepan. Cook and stir over medium heat until mixture comes to full boil. Stir in remaining 2 tablespoons brandy. Unmold steamed pudding. Serve with warm sauce.

MAKES 8 servings

Prep time: 30 minutes
Cooking time: 1½ hours

■ Eggnog Trifle

1¼ cups cold milk
1 package (4-serving size) JELL-O Instant Pudding and Pie Filling, French Vanilla or Vanilla Flavor
¼ cup rum
⅛ teaspoon ground nutmeg
3½ cups (8 ounces) COOL WHIP Whipped Topping, thawed
1 pound cake loaf (about 12 ounces)
2 tablespoons strawberry jam
1 can (11 ounces) mandarin orange sections, drained
1½ cups strawberries, halved
¼ cup sliced almonds, toasted (see page 19 for directions)

POUR milk into medium bowl. Add pudding mix, 2 tablespoons of the rum and nutmeg. Beat with wire whisk until well blended, 1 to 2 minutes. Let stand 5 minutes or until slightly thickened. Fold in ½ of the whipped topping.

CUT rounded top off pound cake; reserve for snacking or another use. Slice remaining cake horizontally into 4 layers. Sprinkle layers evenly with remaining 2 tablespoons rum. Spread jam on surface of 2 layers; top with remaining 2 layers. Cut cakes into 1-inch cubes.

ARRANGE about ½ of the cake cubes on bottom of 2½-quart straight-sided bowl. Spoon ½ of the pudding mixture into bowl. Top with ½ of the fruit and almonds; cover with remaining cake cubes. Spoon remaining pudding mixture over cake. Top with remaining fruit and almonds. Garnish with remaining whipped topping. Chill until ready to serve.

MAKES 8 to 10 servings

Prep time: 30 minutes

■ Sparkling Champagne Dessert

2 packages (4-serving size each) or 1 package (8-serving size) JELL-O Brand Gelatin, Lemon Flavor
2 cups boiling water
2 cups champagne
3 oranges, sectioned
Citrus Curls (see page 18 for directions) (optional)

DISSOLVE gelatin in boiling water. Let stand about 10 minutes to cool. Add champagne. Chill until slightly thickened.

MEASURE 1 cup gelatin into small bowl; set aside. Fold orange sections into remaining gelatin. Spoon into champagne glasses or dessert dishes.

BEAT reserved gelatin at high speed of electric mixer until fluffy, thick and about doubled in volume. Spoon over clear gelatin in glasses. Chill until firm, about 2 hours. Garnish with Citrus Curls, if desired. *MAKES 8 servings*

Prep time: 15 minutes
Chill time: 2 hours

Clockwise from top left: Eggnog Trifle; Sparkling Champagne Dessert; Pink Champagne Sorbet (page 80)

■ Pink Champagne Sorbet

1 package (4-serving size) JELL-O
   Brand Gelatin, Strawberry Flavor
1⅓ cups boiling water
1 bottle (187 mL) pink champagne
¾ cup light corn syrup
2 egg whites, lightly beaten
   Lime slices (optional)

DISSOLVE gelatin in boiling water. Stir in champagne and corn syrup. Beat in egg whites with wire whisk. Pour into 13×9-inch pan. Freeze until firm, about 2 hours.

SPOON ½ of the gelatin mixture into food processor or blender; cover. Process at high speed until smooth but not melted, about 30 seconds. Pour into 9×5-inch loaf pan. Repeat with remaining mixture; pour over mixture in pan. Cover; freeze until firm, about 6 hours or overnight.

SCOOP gelatin mixture into dessert or champagne glasses. Garnish with lime slices, if desired.   *MAKES 8 servings*

NOTE: USE ONLY CLEAN EGGS WITH NO CRACKS IN SHELL.

Prep time: 15 minutes
Freezing time: 8 hours

■ Elegant Raspberry Chocolate Pie

1 package (4-serving size) JELL-O
   Brand Gelatin, Raspberry Flavor
1¼ cups boiling water
1 pint vanilla ice cream, softened
1 packaged chocolate crumb crust
3 tablespoons PARKAY Margarine
2 squares BAKER'S Semi-Sweet
   Chocolate
   COOL WHIP Whipped Topping,
   thawed (optional)
   Raspberries (optional)

DISSOLVE gelatin in boiling water. Spoon in ice cream, stirring until melted and smooth. Chill until slightly thickened, about 10 minutes. Pour into crust. Chill until firm, about 2 hours.

MELT margarine with chocolate; cool. Spread over pie. Chill until chocolate mixture hardens. Garnish with whipped topping and raspberries, if desired.   *MAKES 8 servings*

Note: For ease in serving, let pie stand 5 minutes after spreading on chocolate. With knife, lightly score pie into serving-size pieces. Chill as directed above.

Prep time: 15 minutes
Chill time: 2½ hours

Clockwise from top: Elegant Raspberry Chocolate Pie; Fruit Terrine Supreme (page 82); Raspberry Bavarian (page 83)

■ Fruit Terrine Supreme

2 packages (4-serving size each) or
    1 package (8-serving size)
    JELL-O Brand Gelatin, Lemon
    Flavor
1½ cups boiling water
 ¾ cup orange juice
    Ice cubes
2 teaspoons grated orange rind
3½ cups (8 ounces) COOL WHIP
    Whipped Topping, thawed
 ¼ cup sour cream
 1 tablespoon milk
    Strawberry Sauce (recipe follows)
    Fruit (optional)

DISSOLVE gelatin in boiling water. Combine orange juice and ice cubes to make 1¾ cups. Add to gelatin, stirring until ice is melted. Stir in orange rind. Place bowl in larger bowl of ice and water. Let stand, stirring occasionally, until gelatin is slightly thickened, about 5 minutes.

FOLD whipped topping into gelatin mixture. Spoon into 8×4-inch loaf pan. Chill until firm, at least 3 hours. Unmold onto cutting board.

STIR together sour cream and milk. Spoon about 2 tablespoons of the Strawberry Sauce onto individual dessert plates. Swirl sour cream mixture through Strawberry Sauce to form design (see page 19 for directions). Slice terrine; place in sauce on plates. Garnish with fruit, if desired.   *MAKES 8 to 10 servings*

Strawberry Sauce

2 packages (10 ounces each)
    BIRDS EYE Quick Thaw
    Strawberries, thawed
2 teaspoons cornstarch

PLACE strawberries in food processor or blender; cover. Process until smooth. Combine cornstarch with small amount of the strawberries in medium saucepan; add remaining strawberries. Bring to boil over medium heat, stirring constantly; boil 1 minute. Chill.   *MAKES 2 cups*

Prep time: 30 minutes
Chill time: 3 hours

■ Raspberry Bavarian

1 package (4-serving size) JELL-O
    Brand Gelatin, Raspberry Flavor
¾ cup boiling water
½ cup cold water
    Ice cubes
1¾ cups (4 ounces) COOL WHIP
    Whipped Topping, thawed
    Raspberries (optional)
    Mint leaves (optional)

DISSOLVE gelatin in boiling water. Combine cold water and ice cubes to make 1 cup. Add to gelatin, stirring until ice is melted. Place bowl in larger bowl of ice and water. Let stand, stirring occasionally, until gelatin is slightly thickened, about 5 minutes. Fold in whipped topping.

SPOON gelatin mixture into individual souffle cups with paper collars (see note below). Chill until firm, about 2 hours. Remove collars. Garnish with raspberries and mint leaves, if desired.

MAKES 4 servings

Note: To make collars, cut pieces of waxed paper or foil long enough to wrap around dishes and overlap slightly; fold in half lengthwise. Wrap doubled paper around dish, extending about 1 inch above rim. Secure with tape.

Prep time: 20 minutes
Chill time: 2 hours

■ Valentine Poke Cake

2 baked 9-inch heart-shaped white
    cake layers, cooled
1 package (4-serving size) JELL-O
    Brand Gelatin, Strawberry Flavor
1 cup boiling water
    Pastel Fluffy Topping (recipe
    follows)

PLACE cake layers, top sides up, in 2 clean 9-inch heart-shaped cake pans. Pierce cakes with fork at ½-inch intervals.

DISSOLVE gelatin in boiling water. Carefully pour over cake layers. Chill 3 hours.

DIP cake pans in warm water; unmold. Fill and frost cake with Pastel Fluffy Topping. Garnish with Valentine's Day candies, if desired. Chill until ready to serve.   *MAKES 12 servings*

Pastel Fluffy Topping

1 package (4-serving size) JELL-O
    Brand Gelatin, Strawberry
    Flavor
1 cup boiling water
3½ cups (8 ounces) COOL WHIP
    Whipped Topping, thawed

DISSOLVE gelatin in boiling water. Chill until slightly thickened. Fold in whipped topping.

MAKES about 3½ cups

Prep time: 20 minutes
Chill time: 3 hours

■ Cherry Tart

½ package (15-ounce) refrigerated
    pie crust (1 crust)
1 package (4-serving size) JELL-O
    Pudding and Pie Filling,
    Chocolate Flavor
1¾ cups cold half and half or milk
1 tablespoon cherry liqueur
1 can (21 ounces) cherry pie filling
    COOL WHIP Whipped Topping,
        thawed (optional)
    Chocolate Cutouts (see page 23
        for directions) (optional)

PRESS pastry into 9-inch tart pan.
Pierce bottom with fork. Bake as
directed on package until golden.
Cool on rack.

COMBINE pie filling mix with half and
half in medium saucepan. Cook and
stir over medium heat until mixture
comes to full boil. Stir in liqueur. Cover
surface of pudding with plastic wrap;
cool slightly. Remove plastic wrap.
Pour into tart shell. Chill until set, about
3 hours. Top with cherry pie filling.
Garnish with whipped topping and
Chocolate Cutouts, if desired.

MAKES 8 servings

Prep time: 30 minutes
Chill time: 3 hours

■ St. Patrick's Parfaits

1 package (4-serving size) JELL-O
    Instant Pudding and Pie Filling,
    Pistachio Flavor
2 cups cold milk
    Fudge or chocolate sauce
    COOL WHIP Whipped Topping,
        thawed (optional)
    Chocolate Cutouts (see page 23
        for directions) (optional)

PREPARE pudding mix with milk as
directed on package. Alternately
layer pudding in parfait glasses with
fudge sauce, ending with pudding.
Chill until ready to serve. Garnish with
whipped topping and Chocolate
Cutouts in shamrock shapes, if desired.

MAKES 4 servings

Prep time: 15 minutes

■ Lemon Sour Cream Mold

2 packages (4-serving size each) or
 1 package (8-serving size)
 JELL-O Brand Gelatin, Lemon
 Flavor
2 cups boiling water
1 cup half and half or milk
1 teaspoon vanilla
1 cup (½ pint) sour cream
 Raspberry Sauce (see page 67 for
 recipe) (optional)

DISSOLVE gelatin in boiling water. Add half and half and vanilla; blend in sour cream. (Mixture will appear slightly curdled.) Chill until slightly thickened. Beat until mixture is smooth.

POUR gelatin mixture into 6-cup heart-shaped or ring mold. Chill until firm, about 4 hours. Unmold. Spoon Raspberry Sauce around mold, if desired. *MAKES 12 servings*

Prep time: 15 minutes
Chill time: 4 hours

■ Gelatin Easter Baskets

1 package (4-serving size) JELL-O
 Brand Gelatin, any flavor
1 cup boiling water
½ cup cold water
½ cup BAKER'S ANGEL FLAKE
 Coconut
 Food coloring
 Jelly beans
 Red string licorice

DISSOLVE gelatin in boiling water. Add cold water. Pour into individual ring molds or 6-ounce custard cups. Chill until firm, about 2 hours.

TINT coconut as desired with food coloring (see page 21 for directions).

UNMOLD gelatin onto individual dessert plates. Sprinkle coconut into center of each mold for "grass." Place jelly beans on top of coconut. Cut licorice for basket handles; insert in molds. *MAKES 4 servings*

Prep time: 15 minutes
Chill time: 2 hours

■ Easter Bonnet Cake

1 package (2-layer size) yellow
    cake mix
2 packages (4-serving size each)
    JELL-O Instant Pudding and Pie
    Filling, Lemon Flavor
4 eggs
1 cup water
¼ cup vegetable oil
1½ cups cold milk
3½ cups (8 ounces) COOL WHIP
    Whipped Topping, thawed
2⅔ cups (7 ounces) BAKER'S ANGEL
    FLAKE Coconut
    Cloth ribbon (optional)
    Gumdrop Flowers (see page 20
    for directions) (optional)

COMBINE cake mix, 1 package of the pudding mix, eggs, water and oil in large bowl. Beat at low speed of electric mixer just to moisten, scraping sides of bowl often. Beat at medium speed 4 minutes. Pour 3¼ cups of the batter into greased and floured 1½-quart metal or ovenproof glass bowl; pour remaining batter into greased and floured 12-inch pizza pan. Bake at 350° for 15 minutes for the pan and 50 minutes for the bowl or until cake tester inserted in centers comes out clean.

COOL cakes 10 minutes. Remove from pan and bowl; finish cooling on racks. If necessary, cut thin slice from flat end of bowl-shaped cake so that it will sit flat; split horizontally into 3 layers.

POUR milk into small bowl. Add remaining package of pudding mix. Beat with wire whisk until well blended, 1 to 2 minutes.

PLACE 12-inch cake layer on large serving plate or tray. Spread layer with 1½ cups of the whipped topping. Center bottom layer of bowl-shaped cake on frosted layer; spread with ⅔ of the pudding. Add second layer; spread with remaining pudding. Add top layer, forming the crown.

SPREAD remaining whipped topping over crown. Sprinkle coconut over cake. Tie ribbon around cake crown to form hat band and bow and garnish with Gumdrop Flowers, if desired. Chill until ready to serve.

MAKES 16 servings

Prep time: 45 minutes
Baking time: 50 minutes

*Top: Easter Bonnet Cake; bottom: Gelatin
Easter Baskets (page 85)*

■ Stars and Stripes

1 sheet frozen puff pastry dough
1 egg, lightly beaten
1½ cups cold half and half or milk
1 package (4-serving size) JELL-O Instant Pudding and Pie Filling, French Vanilla or Vanilla Flavor
Blueberries
Raspberries
COOL WHIP Whipped Topping, thawed

THAW puff pastry as directed on package. Unfold pastry to 10×9-inch rectangle. Cut 4 (½-inch) strips from 1 (9-inch) side of rectangle as shown in Diagram 1. (Remaining rectangle will measure 9×8 inches.) Cut 1 inch off each of 2 strips (Diagram 2); discard 1-inch pieces. (You should have 2 8-inch strips and 2 9-inch strips.)

PLACE pastry on baking sheet. Brush with egg. Place strips on top of each side of rectangle to form rim; lightly press strips to base. Brush strips with egg. Pierce bottom of pastry in several places with fork. Chill 20 minutes. Meanwhile, preheat oven to 425°. Bake pastry for 12 to 15 minutes or until golden. (If center of pastry rises, gently press down with fork.) Cool on rack.

POUR half and half into small bowl. Add pudding mix. Beat with wire whisk until well blended, 1 to 2 minutes. Spoon pudding into pastry shell. Chill until set, about 1 hour.

ARRANGE fruit on top of pudding in alternating stripes of blueberries and raspberries. Pipe "stars" of whipped topping around borders.
MAKES 8 to 10 servings

Prep time: 20 minutes
Chill time: 1 hour

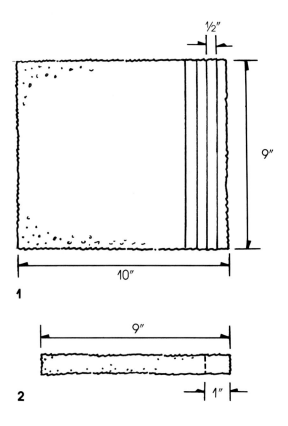

Top: Stars and Stripes; bottom: Lemon Strawberry Stars (page 90)

■ Red-White-and-Blue Salad

1 package (4-serving size) JELL-O
   Brand Gelatin, Strawberry Flavor
1 package (4-serving size) JELL-O
   Brand Gelatin, Black Cherry
   Flavor
3 cups boiling water
1 cup cold water
1 package (4-serving size) JELL-O
   Brand Gelatin, Lemon Flavor
1½ cups sliced strawberries
1 pint vanilla ice cream, softened
1½ cups fresh, frozen or drained
   canned blueberries
   Strawberry Fan (see page 19 for
   directions) (optional)

DISSOLVE strawberry and black cherry gelatins in separate bowls, using 1 cup of the boiling water for each. Add ½ cup cold water to each. Dissolve lemon gelatin in remaining 1 cup boiling water.

PLACE bowl of strawberry gelatin in larger bowl of ice and water. Stir until slightly thickened; add strawberries. Pour into 9×5-inch loaf pan. Chill about 5 minutes.

SPOON ice cream into lemon gelatin, stirring until melted and smooth. Carefully spoon over strawberry gelatin in pan. Chill about 5 minutes.

PLACE bowl of black cherry gelatin in larger bowl of ice and water. Stir until slightly thickened; add blueberries. Carefully spoon over gelatin in pan. Chill until firm, about 6 hours or overnight. Unmold. Garnish with Strawberry Fan, if desired.

MAKES 12 servings

Prep time: 45 minutes
Chill time: 6 hours

■ Lemon Strawberry Stars

1 pound cake loaf (about
   12 ounces)
1 package (4-serving size) JELL-O
   Instant Pudding and Pie Filling,
   Lemon Flavor
2 cups cold milk
   Sliced strawberries
   Strawberry Sauce (see page 82
   for recipe) (optional)

SLICE pound cake horizontally into 5 layers. Cut each layer into 2 star shapes with large cookie cutter. (Reserve cake scraps for snacking or other use.)

PREPARE pudding mix with milk as directed on package.

TOP ½ of the pound cake stars with ½ of the sliced strawberries and ½ of the pudding. Cover with remaining stars, strawberries and pudding. Serve with Strawberry Sauce, if desired.

MAKES 5 servings

Prep time: 15 minutes

Red-White-and-Blue Salad

■ Harvest Pie

1 cup cold milk
1 package (4-serving size) JELL-O Instant Pudding and Pie Filling, French Vanilla or Vanilla Flavor
2 cups thawed COOL WHIP Whipped Topping
1 packaged graham cracker crumb crust
1 apple, chopped
½ cup chopped pecans or walnuts
¼ cup KRAFT Miniature Marshmallows
¼ cup caramel sauce or ice cream topping

POUR milk into medium bowl. Add pie filling mix. Beat with wire whisk until well blended, 1 to 2 minutes. Let stand 1 to 2 minutes or until slightly thickened.

FOLD whipped topping into filling mixture. Pour into crust. Chill until firm, about 2 hours. Sprinkle with apples, pecans and marshmallows just before serving. Drizzle caramel sauce over pie.   *MAKES 8 servings*

Prep time: 15 minutes
Chill time: 2 hours

■ Maple Walnut Cheesecake

⅓ cup PARKAY Margarine
⅓ cup finely chopped walnuts
1 package (11 ounces) JELL-O No Bake Cheesecake mix
1½ cups cold milk
2 tablespoons maple flavor syrup
¼ teaspoon ground cinnamon
¾ cup walnut topping

MELT margarine in small skillet. Add walnuts; cook until lightly toasted, about 3 minutes. Stir in cheesecake crust crumbs. Press crumb mixture onto bottom of 8-inch square pan which has been lined with foil.

MIX milk with cheesecake filling mix, syrup and cinnamon at low speed of electric mixer until well blended. Beat at medium speed 3 minutes. Spread over crust. Chill until firm, at least 1 hour.

HEAT topping just before serving. Cut cheesecake into squares. Serve with warmed topping.
                    MAKES 8 servings

Prep time: 15 minutes
Chill time: 1 hour

Top: Harvest Pie; bottom: Maple Walnut Cheesecake

■ Thanksgiving Cranberry Pie

1 package (15 ounces) refrigerated pie crust (2 crusts)

1 package (4-serving size) JELL-O Brand Gelatin, Orange Flavor or any red flavor

¾ cup boiling water

½ cup orange juice

1 can (8 ounces) jellied or whole berry cranberry sauce

1 teaspoon grated orange rind

1 cup cold half and half or milk

1 package (4-serving size) JELL-O Instant Pudding and Pie Filling, French Vanilla or Vanilla Flavor

1 cup thawed COOL WHIP Whipped Topping

Frosted Cranberries (see page 18 for directions) (optional)

PREPARE and bake 1 sheet of the pie crust in 9-inch pie plate as directed on package; cool. Cut out leaf shapes from remaining sheet of pie crust with small cookie cutter. Place on ungreased baking sheet; bake at 450° for 8 minutes or until golden. Cool.

DISSOLVE gelatin in boiling water. Add orange juice. Place bowl in larger bowl of ice and water. Let stand, stirring occasionally, until gelatin is slightly thickened, about 5 minutes. Stir in cranberry sauce and orange rind. Spoon into pie crust. Chill just until set, about 30 minutes.

POUR half and half into medium bowl. Add pie filling mix. Beat with wire whisk until well blended, 1 to 2 minutes. Let stand 2 minutes or until slightly thickened. Fold in whipped topping. Gently spread over gelatin mixture. Place pastry leaves around rim of pie. Chill until firm, about 2 hours. Garnish with additional whipped topping and Frosted Cranberries, if desired.

MAKES 8 servings

Prep time: 30 minutes
Baking time: 20 minutes
Chill time: 2½ hours

■ Pumpkin Flan

1 package (4½ ounces) JELL-O AMERICANA Custard Mix*

2½ cups milk

2 teaspoons grated orange rind

¼ teaspoon ground cinnamon

1 egg yolk

1 cup canned pumpkin

Citrus Fan (see page 18 for directions) (optional)

Mint leaves (optional)

COMBINE custard mix, milk, orange rind and cinnamon in medium saucepan; mix in egg yolk. Cook, stirring constantly, over medium-low heat until mixture comes to full boil. Remove from heat. Add pumpkin, stirring until well mixed. Pour into 1½-quart souffle dish or bowl. Chill until firm, about 3 hours.

DIP flan in hot water; unmold onto serving plate. Garnish with Citrus Fan and mint leaves, if desired.

MAKES 8 servings

*1 package (4-serving size) JELL-O Pudding and Pie Filling, Vanilla Flavor, may be substituted for the custard mix.

Prep time: 15 minutes
Chill time: 3 hours

Top: Pumpkin Flan; bottom: Thanksgiving Cranberry Pie

■ Frozen Pumpkin Pie

1 package (6-serving size) JELL-O Instant Pudding and Pie Filling, French Vanilla or Vanilla Flavor
1 can (16 ounces) pumpkin
1 cup cold milk
½ teaspoon ground cinnamon*
¼ teaspoon ground nutmeg*
¼ teaspoon ground ginger*
1¾ cups (4 ounces) COOL WHIP Whipped Topping, thawed
1 baked 9-inch pie shell or graham cracker crumb crust, cooled

COMBINE pie filling mix, pumpkin, milk and spices in medium bowl. Mix at low speed of electric mixer until just blended, about 1 minute. Fold in whipped topping. Spoon into pie shell. Freeze until firm, about 4 hours or overnight.

LET pie stand at room temperature about 30 minutes before cutting to serve. Garnish with additional whipped topping, if desired.
MAKES 8 servings

*1 teaspoon pumpkin pie spice may be substituted for cinnamon, nutmeg and ginger.

Prep time: 15 minutes
Freezing time: 4 hours

■ Pumpkin Cream Pie

1 package (6-serving size) JELL-O Pudding and Pie Filling, French Vanilla or Vanilla Flavor
3 tablespoons sugar
½ teaspoon ground cinnamon*
¼ teaspoon ground nutmeg*
¼ teaspoon ground ginger*
1¾ cups milk**
1 egg, slightly beaten
1 cup canned pumpkin
1 baked 9-inch pie shell or graham cracker crumb crust, cooled

COMBINE pie filling mix, sugar, spices, milk, egg and pumpkin in medium saucepan. Cook and stir over medium heat until mixture comes to full boil. Remove from heat. Cool 5 minutes, stirring twice.

POUR pie filling into pie shell. Chill 4 hours. Garnish with whipped topping and pecan halves or chopped nuts, if desired.   *MAKES 8 servings*

*1 teaspoon pumpkin pie spice may be substituted for cinnamon, nutmeg and ginger.

**1 can (13 ounces) evaporated milk may be substituted for 1¾ cups milk.

Prep time: 25 minutes
Chill time: 4 hours

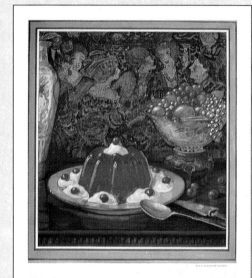

JELL-O

AMERICA'S MOST FAMOUS DESSERT
Circa 1915

FESTIVE CELEBRATIONS

▦ Lemon Cheese Tart

**2 packages (11 ounces each)
JELL-O No Bake Cheesecake
mix**
¼ cup sugar
⅔ cup PARKAY Margarine, melted
**2 packages (4-serving size each) or
1 package (8-serving size)
JELL-O Brand Gelatin, Lemon
Flavor**
2 cups boiling water
1 cup cold water
3 cups cold milk
**1½ teaspoons grated lemon rind
(optional)**
**1 cup (about) seedless red or
green grapes, halved
Mint leaves**

MIX cheesecake crust crumbs with sugar in 9-inch springform pan. Stir in margarine. Press crumb mixture firmly onto bottom of pan.

DISSOLVE gelatin in boiling water. Add cold water. Chill until slightly thickened.

MIX milk with cheesecake filling mix and lemon rind at low speed of electric mixer until blended. Beat at medium speed 3 minutes. Pour over crust. Arrange grape halves on top of cheesecake to resemble large grape cluster. Place mint leaves at stem end of cluster. Carefully spoon thickened gelatin over grape cluster and filling. Chill until set, about 3 hours. Run hot metal spatula or knife around edge of pan before removing sides of pan.

MAKES 12 servings

Note: This recipe may be prepared 1 day ahead.

Prep time: 30 minutes
Chill time: 3 hours

Clockwise from top left: Lemon Cheese Tart; Sparkling Punch Bowl (page 100); Almond Heart Napoleons (page 100)

■ Almond Heart Napoleons

1 package (17¼ ounces) frozen
    puff pastry sheets
1¼ cups cold half and half or milk
2 tablespoons almond liqueur*
1 package (4-serving size) JELL-O
    Instant Pudding and Pie Filling,
    French Vanilla or Vanilla Flavor
½ cup confectioners sugar
2 teaspoons (about) hot water
1 square BAKER'S Semi-Sweet
    Chocolate, melted

THAW puff pastry as directed on
package. Preheat oven to 350°.
Unfold pastry. Using 2-inch heart-
shaped cookie cutter, cut each sheet
into 12 hearts. Bake on ungreased
baking sheets for 20 minutes or until
golden. Remove from baking sheets.
Cool on racks. When pastry is
completely cooled, split each heart
horizontally in half.

POUR half and half and liqueur into
small bowl. Add pudding mix. Beat
with wire whisk until well blended, 1 to
2 minutes. Chill 10 minutes.

SPREAD about 1 tablespoon of the
pudding mixture onto bottom half of
each pastry; top with remaining
pastry half.

STIR together confectioners sugar and
hot water in small bowl to make thin
glaze. Spread over hearts. (If glaze
becomes too thick, add more hot
water until glaze is of desired
consistency.) Before glaze dries, drizzle
chocolate on top to form thin lines.
Draw wooden pick through chocolate
to make design. Chill until ready to
serve.   *MAKES 2 dozen pastries*

Prep time: 30 minutes
Baking time: 20 minutes

*½ teaspoon almond extract may be
substituted for 2 tablespoons almond
liqueur.

■ Sparkling Punch Bowl

8 packages (4-serving size each) or
    4 packages (8-serving size
    each) JELL-O Brand Gelatin, any
    flavor
8 cups boiling water
1 bottle (1 liter) ginger ale
    Ice cubes
5 cups cut-up fruit*
1 can (20 ounces) pineapple
    chunks in juice, drained
    Mint leaves (optional)

DISSOLVE gelatin in boiling water.
Combine ginger ale and ice cubes to
make 8 cups. Add to gelatin, stirring
until slightly thickened. Remove any
unmelted ice. Measure 4 cups of the
gelatin; set aside. Fold cut-up fruit and
pineapple chunks into remaining
gelatin. Pour into large punch bowl.
Chill until set but not firm.

WHIP reserved gelatin at high speed
of electric mixer until fluffy, thick and
about doubled in volume. Spoon over
gelatin in punch bowl. Chill until firm,
about 2 hours. Garnish with additional
fruit and mint leaves, if desired.
        MAKES 32 servings

*We suggest sliced bananas,
strawberries or grapes.

Note: If large punch bowl is not
available, use smaller bowl and pour
extra gelatin mixture into punch cups.

Prep time: 20 minutes
Chill time: 2 hours

■ Continental Cheese Mold

1 package (4-serving size) JELL-O
   Brand Gelatin, Orange or
   Lemon Flavor
¾ cup boiling water
1 container (16 ounces) cottage
   cheese
2 ounces Roquefort or bleu cheese,
   crumbled
½ cup sour cream
1 teaspoon seasoned salt
1 teaspoon lemon juice
1 teaspoon Worcestershire sauce
2 tablespoons chopped parsley
   Sliced carrots (optional)
   Watercress (optional)
   Assorted crackers and fresh
      vegetables

DISSOLVE gelatin in boiling water.
Combine cheeses, sour cream,
seasoned salt, lemon juice and
Worcestershire sauce in large bowl;
beat until smooth. (Or, combine in
blender and blend until smooth.)
Gradually blend in gelatin. Add
parsley. Pour into 4-cup mold or bowl.
Chill until set, about 3 hours. Unmold.
Garnish with carrot slices and
watercress, if desired. Serve with
assorted crackers and vegetables.

MAKES 4 cups

Prep time: 15 minutes
Chill time: 3 hours

■ Lemon Berry Terrine

1 pound cake loaf (about
    12 ounces)
1 package (8 ounces)
    PHILADELPHIA BRAND Cream
    Cheese, softened
2 cups cold milk
1 package (4-serving size) JELL-O
    Instant Pudding and Pie Filling,
    Lemon Flavor
1 teaspoon grated lemon rind
3½ cups (8 ounces) COOL WHIP
    Whipped Topping, thawed
1 pint strawberries, stems removed

LINE bottom and sides of 8×4-inch loaf
pan with waxed paper.

CUT rounded top off pound cake;
reserve for snacking or other use. Trim
crusts from pound cake. Cut cake
horizontally into 5 slices. Line bottom
and long sides of loaf pan with 3 cake
slices. Cut another cake slice in half;
place on short sides of pan.

BEAT cream cheese at medium speed
of electric mixer until smooth.
Gradually beat in 1 cup of the milk.
Add pudding mix, remaining 1 cup
milk and lemon rind. Beat at low
speed until blended, 1 to 2 minutes.
Fold in 1½ cups of the whipped
topping.

SPOON ½ of the filling into loaf pan.
Reserve several strawberries for
garnish. Arrange remaining
strawberries in filling, pressing down
slightly. Top with remaining filling. Place
remaining cake slice on top of filling.
Chill until firm, about 3 hours.

UNMOLD dessert onto serving plate;
remove waxed paper. Garnish with
remaining whipped topping and
strawberries.   *MAKES 16 servings*

Prep time: 30 minutes
Chill time: 3 hours

■ Apricot Pear Tart

1⅓ cups shortbread cookie or
    graham cracker crumbs
2 tablespoons sugar
¼ cup PARKAY Margarine, melted
1 package (4-serving size) JELL-O
    Brand Gelatin, Apricot Flavor
1 cup boiling water
⅔ cup cold water
1¾ cups (4 ounces) COOL WHIP
    Whipped Topping, thawed
½ teaspoon ground ginger
1 can (16 ounces) pear halves,
    drained
    Mint leaves
    Cinnamon stick, cut into ¾-inch
    pieces

MIX together cookie crumbs, sugar
and margarine in small bowl. Press
crumb mixture onto bottom of 9-inch
springform pan.

DISSOLVE gelatin in boiling water. Add
cold water. Measure ¾ cup gelatin;
set aside. Chill remaining gelatin until
slightly thickened. Fold in whipped
topping and ginger. Spoon over crust.

CHILL measured gelatin until slightly
thickened. Slice pears lengthwise,
cutting almost through stem ends;
arrange on whipped topping mixture
in pan, fanning each one slightly (see
page 19 for directions). Place mint leaf
and cinnamon stick at stem end of
each pear. Carefully spoon thickened
gelatin over pears and filling. Chill until
firm, about 3 hours. Run hot metal
spatula or knife around edge of pan
before removing sides of pan.
                    MAKES 12 servings

Prep time: 30 minutes
Chill time: 3 hours

*Clockwise from top: Apricot Pear Tart;
Jell-O Creamy Jigglers (page 146);
Lemon Berry Terrine*

■ Ginger Berry Bells

2 cans (16 ounces each) pear
  halves in syrup, undrained
4 packages (4-serving size each) or
  2 packages (8-serving size
  each) JELL-O Brand Gelatin,
  Strawberry Flavor
1½ cups ginger ale
1 container (16 ounces) vanilla
  yogurt
1 pint strawberries, quartered

DRAIN pears, reserving syrup. Dice
pears; set aside. Add enough water to
syrup to make 3 cups. Bring to boil.
Completely dissolve gelatin in boiling
liquid. Add ginger ale. Measure 4 cups
of the gelatin mixture into large bowl;
chill until thickened. Stir remaining
gelatin into yogurt until smooth. Divide
mixture between 2 (5-cup) bell-
shaped molds. Chill until set but not
firm.

FOLD pears and strawberries into
thickened gelatin. Divide mixture;
spoon over yogurt mixture in molds.
Chill until firm, about 3 hours. Unmold
onto serving platter; position to
resemble "wedding bells."

MAKES 20 servings

Note: Any 5-cup mold may be
substituted for bell-shaped mold.

Prep time: 30 minutes
Chill time: 3 hours

■ Orange Crepes Suzette

6 tablespoons PARKAY Margarine
1 package (11 ounces) JELL-O No
  Bake Cheesecake mix
1½ cups cold milk
2 teaspoons grated orange rind
16 crepes (homemade or
  commercial)
⅔ cup orange juice
¼ cup sugar
¼ cup orange liqueur

MELT 2 tablespoons of the margarine.
Stir in cheesecake crust crumbs until
well mixed; set aside.

MIX milk with cheesecake filling mix
and 1 teaspoon of the orange rind at
low speed of electric mixer until
blended. Beat at medium speed
3 minutes. Spread each crepe with
about 3 tablespoons of the
cheesecake filling; sprinkle with
1 tablespoon crumb mixture. Fold into
quarters; arrange on shallow serving
platter.

MIX together orange juice, sugar,
remaining margarine and orange rind
in small saucepan. Add liqueur; bring
to simmer. Spoon sauce over crepes.
Garnish with Citrus Curls (see page 18
for directions), if desired.

MAKES 8 servings

Prep time: 20 minutes

■ Shrimp Spread

- **1 package (4-serving size) JELL-O Brand Gelatin, Lemon Flavor**
- **1 cup boiling water**
- **1 package (8 ounces) PHILADELPHIA BRAND Cream Cheese, softened**
- **1 cup (½ pint) sour cream**
- **½ cup MIRACLE WHIP Salad Dressing**
- **⅓ cup chili sauce**
- **3 tablespoons prepared horseradish**
- **1 teaspoon Worcestershire sauce**
- **1 package (6 ounces) frozen cooked shrimp, thawed, drained and chopped**
- **Assorted crackers and fresh vegetables**

DISSOLVE gelatin in boiling water. Beat cream cheese in large bowl at medium speed of electric mixer until smooth. Add sour cream, salad dressing, chili sauce, horseradish and Worcestershire sauce; beat until well blended. Stir in shrimp. Gradually stir in gelatin. Pour into 5-cup mold. Chill until firm, about 4 hours. Unmold. Serve with crackers and vegetables.

MAKES 5 cups

Prep time: 20 minutes
Chill time: 4 hours

■ Raspberry Sorbet

- **1 package (10 ounces) BIRDS EYE Quick Thaw Red Raspberries, thawed**
- **1 cup cold water**
- **1 package (4-serving size) JELL-O Brand Gelatin, Raspberry Flavor**
- **1 cup sugar**
- **2 cups boiling water**

PLACE raspberries and cold water in blender; cover. Blend at high speed until smooth. Strain to remove seeds.

DISSOLVE gelatin and sugar in boiling water. Add raspberry puree. Pour into 9-inch square pan. Freeze until ice crystals form 1 inch around edge, about 1 hour.

SPOON gelatin mixture into chilled blender container; cover. Blend at high speed until smooth, about 30 seconds. Return mixture to pan. Freeze until firm, about 6 hours or overnight.   *MAKES 10 servings*

Prep time: 20 minutes
Freezing time: 7 hours

■ Fruit-Topped Lemon Cheese Squares

15 whole graham crackers, broken in half
2 packages (8 ounces each) PHILADELPHIA BRAND Cream Cheese, softened
3 cups cold milk
2 packages (6-serving size each) JELL-O Instant Pudding and Pie Filling, Lemon Flavor
1¾ cups (4 ounces) COOL WHIP Whipped Topping, thawed
1 can (21 ounces) pie filling, any fruit flavor

ARRANGE ½ of the crackers on bottom of 13×9-inch pan, cutting crackers to fit, if necessary.

BEAT cream cheese at low speed of electric mixer until smooth. Gradually beat in 1 cup of the milk. Add pudding mix and remaining milk. Beat at low speed until well blended, 1 to 2 minutes. Fold in whipped topping.

SPREAD ½ of the pudding mixture over crackers. Add second layer of crackers; top with remaining pudding mixture. Freeze 2 hours. Let stand at room temperature 15 minutes before cutting into squares. Spoon pie filling over each square.

MAKES 18 servings

Prep time: 20 minutes
Freezing time: 2 hours

Clockwise from top left: Fruit-Topped Lemon Cheese Squares; Pineapple Bombe; Fruity Cheese Spread (page 108)

■ Pineapple Bombe

2 cans (20 ounces each) pineapple slices, drained
8 maraschino cherries, stemmed and halved
2½ cups cold milk
2 packages (4-serving size each) JELL-O Instant Pudding and Pie Filling, French Vanilla or Vanilla Flavor
3½ cups (8 ounces) COOL WHIP Whipped Topping, thawed
1 pound cake loaf (about 12 ounces), cut into 14 slices

LINE 2-quart bowl with plastic wrap. Arrange about 16 pineapple slices on bottom and sides of lined bowl, pushing slices as closely together as possible. Place cherry half, cut side up, in center of each pineapple slice.

POUR milk into large bowl. Add pudding mix. Beat with wire whisk until well blended, 1 to 2 minutes. Let stand 5 minutes. Fold in ½ of the whipped topping.

SPREAD about ⅓ of the pudding mixture over pineapple in bowl. Place about 6 cake slices over pudding layer; press down gently. Arrange 5 pineapple slices over cake slices. Layer with ⅓ of the pudding mixture, 4 cake slices and remaining pineapple. Cover with remaining pudding; top with remaining cake slices. Press down gently. Cover with plastic wrap. Chill at least 1 hour.

INVERT dessert onto serving platter. Carefully remove plastic wrap. Garnish with remaining whipped topping.

MAKES 16 servings

Prep time: 30 minutes
Chill time: 1 hour

■ Fruity Cheese Spread

2 packages (8 ounces each)
   PHILADELPHIA BRAND Cream
   Cheese, softened
1 package (4-serving size) JELL-O
   Brand Gelatin, any flavor
¼ cup chopped pecans
   Assorted fresh fruit, cookies and
   crackers*

BEAT cream cheese in large bowl until
smooth. Beat in gelatin until well
blended. Form mixture into 5-inch
round. Cover with plastic wrap. Chill
about 1 hour.

REMOVE plastic wrap. Press pecans
gently around edges of cheese round.
Serve with fruit, cookies and crackers.

MAKES 2 cups

*We suggest sliced apples or pears,
grapes and strawberries.

Note: Cheese round may be made 2
days ahead and refrigerated; let
stand at room temperature 15 minutes
before serving.

Prep time: 15 minutes
Chill time: 1 hour

■ Strawberry-Peach Upside-Down Cake

1 can (29 ounces) sliced peaches,
   drained*
1 package (4-serving size) JELL-O
   Brand Gelatin, Strawberry Flavor
1 package (4-serving size) JELL-O
   Brand Gelatin, Peach Flavor
1 teaspoon ground cinnamon
   (optional)
3 tablespoons PARKAY Margarine
1 package (2-layer size) yellow
   cake mix

ARRANGE peaches on bottom of
greased 13x9-inch pan. Combine
strawberry and peach flavor gelatins
and cinnamon in small bowl. Sprinkle
about ¾ of the gelatin mixture evenly
over peaches; dot with margarine.

PREPARE cake mix as directed on
package. Pour ¾ of the batter over
peaches in pan. Stir remaining gelatin
mixture into remaining cake batter
until well blended. Pour over batter in
pan. Swirl spatula through batter to
marble. Bake at 350° for 45 minutes or
until cake tester inserted in center
comes out clean. Cool in pan 5
minutes. Invert onto serving platter;
finish cooling. Serve warm with
whipped topping, if desired.

MAKES 18 servings

*2 cups sliced peeled fresh peaches
may be substituted for canned
peaches.

Prep time: 20 minutes
Baking time: 45 minutes

■ Chili Ham and Cheese Spread

1 package (4-serving size) JELL-O Brand Gelatin, Lemon Flavor
1 cup boiling water
1 package (8 ounces) PHILADELPHIA BRAND Cream Cheese, softened
2 cups (1 pint) sour cream
¼ cup chili sauce
1 teaspoon Worcestershire sauce
1 can (4¼ ounces) deviled ham
1 can (4 ounces) chopped green chilies, drained
  Cilantro or flat parsley (optional)
  Tomato wedges (optional)
  Tortilla chips, assorted crackers and fresh vegetables

DISSOLVE gelatin in boiling water. Beat cream cheese in large bowl at medium speed of electric mixer until smooth. Add sour cream, chili sauce and Worcestershire sauce; beat until well blended. Stir in deviled ham and chilies. Gradually stir in gelatin. Pour into 5-cup mold. Chill until firm, about 4 hours. Unmold. Garnish with cilantro and tomato wedges, if desired. Serve with tortilla chips, crackers and vegetables.   *MAKES 5 cups*

Prep time: 15 minutes
Chill time: 4 hours

■ Snack Mix

4 cups popped popcorn
2 cups thin pretzel sticks
2 cups crisp corn cereal squares
1 cup peanuts
½ cup raisins
6 tablespoons PARKAY Margarine, melted
1 package (4-serving size) JELL-O Brand Gelatin, any flavor

PLACE popcorn, pretzels, cereal, peanuts and raisins in large bowl. Add margarine; toss to coat well. Sprinkle with gelatin; toss until evenly coated.

MAKES 10 cups

Prep time: 10 minutes

■ Winner's Circle Layered Dessert

4½ cups cold milk
3 packages (4-serving size each) JELL-O Instant Pudding and Pie Filling, French Vanilla or Vanilla Flavor
1¾ cups (4 ounces) COOL WHIP Whipped Topping, thawed
4 packages (4-serving size each) or 2 packages (8-serving size each) JELL-O Brand Gelatin, Strawberry Flavor
3 cups boiling water
2 cups cold water
Ice cubes
2 cups blueberries
2 cups sliced strawberries

POUR milk into large bowl. Add pudding mix. Beat with wire whisk until well blended, 1 to 2 minutes. Let stand 5 minutes. Fold in 1 cup of the whipped topping; chill.

DISSOLVE ½ of the gelatin in 1½ cups of the boiling water. Combine 1 cup of the cold water and ice cubes to make 1½ cups. Add to dissolved gelatin, stirring until slightly thickened. Remove any unmelted ice. Stir in ½ of the blueberries and strawberries. Spoon into 4-quart bowl. Chill 15 minutes or until thickened. Meanwhile, prepare remaining gelatin as directed above. Stir in remaining fruit.

TOP gelatin mixture in serving bowl with ½ of the pudding mixture, then remaining gelatin mixture. Chill 15 minutes or until thickened. Top with remaining pudding mixture. Chill until firm, about 3 hours. Garnish with remaining whipped topping and additional fruit, if desired.

MAKES 32 servings

Prep time: 30 minutes
Chill time: 4 hours

Clockwise from top left: Winner's Circle Layered Dessert; Snack Mix; Mitt Cut-Up Cake (page 112) and Jell-O Jigglers (page 143)

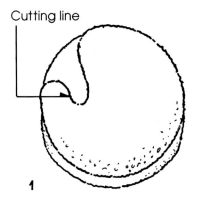

Cutting line

1

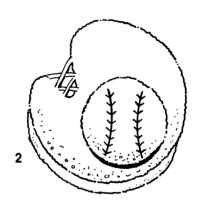

2

■ Mitt Cut-Up Cake

1 package (2-layer size) yellow
    cake mix
1 cup cold milk
1 package (4-serving size) JELL-O
    Instant Pudding and Pie Filling,
    Chocolate or Chocolate Fudge
    Flavor
3½ cups (8 ounces) COOL WHIP
    Whipped Topping, thawed
    Chocolate sprinkles
    String licorice
    JELL-O Jigglers (see page 143
    for recipe) (optional)

PREPARE cake mix as directed on
package. Pour 2 cups of the batter
into greased and floured 1-quart
ovenproof bowl; pour remaining
batter into greased and floured 9-inch
round cake pan. Bake at 325° for 50
minutes or until cake tester inserted in
centers comes out clean. Cool 15
minutes. Remove from pan and bowl;
finish cooling on racks. Cut cake as
shown in Diagram 1.

POUR milk into medium bowl. Add
pudding mix. Beat with wire whisk until
well blended, 1 to 2 minutes. Fold in
2½ cups of the whipped topping.

SPREAD pudding mixture over sides
and top of 9-inch layer. Use remaining
whipped topping to cover bowl-
shaped cake; place over 9-inch layer.
Decorate with chocolate sprinkles
and licorice to resemble mitt and ball
(Diagram 2). Chill cake until ready to
serve. Arrange star-shaped Jigglers
around cake, if desired.

MAKES 12 servings

Prep time: 30 minutes
Baking time: 50 minutes

■ Double Chocolate Football Cake

1 package (2-layer size) chocolate cake mix
1 package (4-serving size) JELL-O Instant Pudding and Pie Filling, Chocolate or Chocolate Fudge Flavor
4 eggs
1 cup water
¼ cup vegetable oil
  Easy Creamy Frosting (recipe follows)
  String licorice
  Candy corn
  BAKER'S Semi-Sweet Real Chocolate Chips

COMBINE cake mix, pudding mix, eggs, water and oil in large bowl. Blend at low speed of electric mixer just to moisten, scraping sides of bowl often. Beat at medium speed 4 minutes. Pour into greased and floured 9-inch square pan. Bake at 325° for 50 to 55 minutes or until cake tester inserted in center comes out clean and cake begins to pull away from sides of pan. (Do not underbake.) Cool in pan 15 minutes. Remove from pan; finish cooling on rack.

PLACE cake, right-side up, on large cutting board. Cut as shown in Diagram 1, reserving outside corners. Spread frosting over cake, mounding in center for rounded appearance. Crumble reserved cake pieces; sprinkle over frosted cake. Decorate with licorice and candies to resemble football (Diagram 2). Chill until ready to serve.   *MAKES 12 servings*

Easy Creamy Frosting

⅓ cup cold milk
1 package (4-serving size) JELL-O Instant Pudding, Chocolate or Chocolate Fudge Flavor
1 teaspoon vanilla
⅓ cup PARKAY Margarine, softened
3 cups confectioners sugar

POUR milk into large bowl. Add pudding mix and vanilla; mix until smooth. Add margarine; blend well. Gradually blend in sugar, beating until smooth. (If mixture becomes too thick, add milk until frosting is of desired consistency.)   *MAKES about 2 cups*

Prep time: 30 minutes
Baking time: 50 minutes

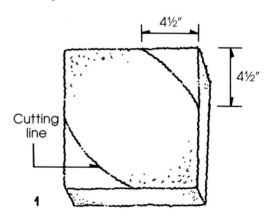

1

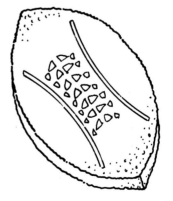

2

■ Chocolate Berry Torte

1 package (2-layer size) chocolate cake mix

1 package (4-serving size) JELL-O Instant Pudding and Pie Filling, Chocolate or Chocolate Fudge Flavor

4 eggs

1 cup water

¼ cup vegetable oil

3 cups cold milk

2 tablespoons chocolate or coffee liqueur (optional)

2 packages (4-serving size each) JELL-O Instant Pudding and Pie Filling, French Vanilla or Vanilla Flavor

1¾ cups (4 ounces) COOL WHIP Whipped Topping, thawed

2 pints strawberries

COMBINE cake mix, chocolate pudding mix, eggs, water and oil in large bowl. Blend at low speed of electric mixer just to moisten, scraping sides of bowl often. Beat at medium speed 4 minutes. Pour into 2 greased and floured 9-inch round cake pans. Bake at 350° for 35 to 40 minutes or until cake tester inserted in centers comes out clean. Cool in pans 15 minutes. Remove from pans; finish cooling on racks.

POUR milk and liqueur into large bowl. Add vanilla pudding mix. Beat with wire whisk until well blended, 1 to 2 minutes. Let stand 5 minutes. Fold in whipped topping. Chill 15 minutes.

CUT each cake layer in half horizontally. Reserve a few strawberries for garnish; slice remaining strawberries. Place 1 cake layer on serving plate; top with ¼ of the pudding mixture and ⅓ of the sliced strawberries. Repeat layers, using remaining cake, pudding mixture and sliced strawberries, ending with pudding mixture. Chill at least 1 hour. Garnish with reserved strawberries.

MAKES 12 servings

Prep time: 30 minutes
Baking time: 35 minutes
Chill time: 1 hour

Chocolate Berry Torte

■ Happy Birthday Dessert

1 package (4-serving size) JELL-O Brand Gelatin, any flavor except lemon
5 cups boiling water
2¼ cups cold water
4 packages (4-serving size each) or 2 packages (8-serving size each) JELL-O Brand Gelatin, Lemon Flavor
1 pint vanilla ice cream, softened COOL WHIP Whipped Topping, thawed (optional)

DISSOLVE 1 package gelatin (not lemon) in 1 cup of the boiling water. Add ¼ cup of the cold water. Pour into 9-inch square pan. Chill until firm.

DISSOLVE lemon gelatin in remaining 4 cups boiling water. Remove 2 cups gelatin and mix with remaining 2 cups cold water; chill until slightly thickened. Spoon ice cream into remaining gelatin, stirring until melted and smooth. Pour into 13x9-inch baking dish or pan. Chill until set but not firm. Top with clear lemon gelatin. Chill until set, about 3 hours.

CUT gelatin in 9-inch pan with alphabet cookie cutters to spell "Happy Birthday." (Cut remaining gelatin into cubes; reserve for snacking or other use.) Carefully transfer cutouts to top of gelatin. Garnish with whipped topping, if desired. _MAKES 18 servings_

Prep time: 30 minutes
Chill time: 3 hours

■ Pineapple Party Cake

1 package (4-serving size) JELL-O Brand Gelatin, Orange Flavor
¾ cup boiling water
1 can (8 ounces) crushed pineapple in juice, undrained
1½ cups ice cubes
2 baked 9-inch yellow or white cake layers, cooled
3½ cups (8 ounces) COOL WHIP Whipped Topping, thawed

DISSOLVE gelatin in boiling water. Add pineapple and ice cubes. Stir until gelatin begins to thicken, 3 to 5 minutes. Remove any unmelted ice. Chill until thickened.

SPOON 1 cup thickened gelatin over each cake layer; chill about 15 minutes.

FOLD whipped topping into remaining gelatin mixture. (If mixture becomes too thick, add milk until frosting is of desired consistency.)

PLACE 1 cake layer, gelatin side up, on serving plate. Top with second cake layer, gelatin side up. Frost sides and about 1 inch around top edge of cake with whipped topping mixture. Chill until ready to serve.
MAKES 12 servings

Prep time: 30 minutes
Chill time: 1 hour

Clockwise from top left: Happy Birthday Dessert; Pineapple Party Cake; Butterfly Cupcakes (page 118)

◼ Butterfly Cupcakes

1 cup cold milk
1 package (4-serving size) JELL-O
    Instant Pudding and Pie Filling,
    any flavor
3½ cups (8 ounces) COOL WHIP
    Whipped Topping, thawed
 24 cupcakes
    Sprinkles
    Pastel confetti candies
    Black string licorice, cut into
    2-inch strips

POUR milk into medium bowl. Add pudding mix. Beat with wire whisk until well blended, 1 to 2 minutes. Fold in whipped topping. Reserve 1 teaspoon pudding mixture.

CUT tops off cupcakes. Cut each top in half; set aside. Spoon 2 heaping tablespoons pudding mixture onto each cupcake; top with sprinkles. For each cupcake, insert 2 top halves of cupcake, cut sides together, in pudding mixture, raising outside ends slightly to resemble butterfly wings. Lightly dip confetti candies into reserved pudding mixture; arrange on cupcake wings. Insert string licorice in pudding mixture to resemble antennae. Chill until ready to serve.

MAKES 2 dozen cupcakes

Prep time: 25 minutes

◼ Graduation Book Cake

1 package (2-layer size) white cake
    mix
1 package (4-serving size) JELL-O
    Instant Pudding and Pie Filling,
    Vanilla Flavor
4 eggs
1 cup water
¼ cup vegetable oil
3½ cups (8 ounces) COOL WHIP
    Whipped Topping, thawed
    Prepared decorating icing in tube
    (any color)
    Berry Cream Sauce (see page 34
    for recipe) (optional)

COMBINE cake mix, pudding mix, eggs, water and oil in large bowl. Beat at low speed of electric mixer just to moisten, scraping sides of bowl often. Beat at medium speed 4 minutes. Pour into greased and floured 13×9-inch pan. Bake at 350° for 45 to 50 minutes or until cake tester inserted in center comes out clean and cake begins to pull away from sides of pan. (Do not underbake.) Cool cake in pan 15 minutes. Remove from pan; finish cooling on rack.

PLACE cake, top-side down, on large tray. Make ¾-inch deep cut down center of cake; cut and remove 2 wedge-shaped pieces. Round off short edges of cake to resemble an open book. Frost cake with whipped topping. Decorate with decorating icing. Chill until ready to serve. Serve with Berry Cream Sauce, if desired.

MAKES 18 servings

Prep time: 30 minutes
Baking time: 45 minutes

Circa 1940

FUN FOR CHILDREN

Pitcher's Mounds

1 package (4-serving size) JELL-O
    Instant Pudding and Pie Filling,
    Chocolate Flavor
2 cups cold milk
3½ cups (8 ounces) COOL WHIP
    Whipped Topping, thawed
1 package (16 ounces) chocolate
    sandwich cookies, crushed
8 to 10 (8-ounce) paper or plastic
    cups

PREPARE pudding mix with milk as
directed on package. Let stand 5
minutes. Fold in whipped topping and
½ of the crushed cookies.

PLACE about 1 tablespoon crushed
cookies in each cup. Fill cups about ¾
full with pudding mixture. Top with
remaining crushed cookies. Chill until
set, about 1 hour. Place toy sports
figure in center of each "mound," if
desired.   *MAKES 8 to 10 servings*

Prep time: 15 minutes
Chill time: 1 hour

Microwave Popcorn Balls

¼ cup (½ stick) PARKAY Margarine
1 bag (10½ ounces) KRAFT
    Miniature Marshmallows
1 package (4-serving size) JELL-O
    Brand Gelatin, any flavor
12 cups popped popcorn
1 cup peanuts (optional)

COMBINE margarine and
marshmallows in large microwavable
bowl. Microwave on HIGH 1½ to 2
minutes or until marshmallows are
puffed. Add gelatin; stir until well
blended. Pour marshmallow mixture
over combined popcorn and
peanuts. Stir to coat well. Shape into
balls or other shapes with greased
hands.   *MAKES about 2 dozen
popcorn balls*

Prep time: 10 minutes

*Clockwise from top left: Gelatin Tilt (page
122) and JELL-O Jigglers (page 143);
Pitcher's Mounds; Microwave Popcorn
Balls; "Out of the Park"
Pudding-Wiches (page 122)*

"Out of the Park" Pudding-Wiches

½ cup peanut butter
1½ cups cold milk
1 package (4-serving size) JELL-O Instant Pudding and Pie Filling, any flavor
Assorted cookies
Sprinkles (optional)

STIR peanut butter in small bowl until smooth. Gradually stir in milk. Add pudding mix. Beat with wire whisk or at low speed of electric mixer until well blended, 1 to 2 minutes.

SPREAD pudding mixture about ½ inch thick on cookie. Top with second cookie, pressing cookies together lightly and smoothing edges of pudding mixture with spatula. Coat edges with sprinkles, if desired. Repeat making sandwiches with remaining cookies and filling. Freeze until firm, about 3 hours.

MAKES about 2 dozen pudding-wiches

Note: Pudding-wiches can be wrapped and stored in freezer up to 2 weeks.

Prep time: 15 minutes
Freezing time: 3 hours

Gelatin Tilt

1 package (4-serving size) JELL-O Brand Gelatin, any flavor
COOL WHIP Whipped Topping, thawed (optional)
Jigglers (see page 143 for recipe) (optional)

PREPARE gelatin as directed on package. Measure ⅔ cup gelatin into small bowl; chill until slightly thickened Pour remaining gelatin into parfait or any stemmed glasses, filling each glass about ½ full. Tilt glasses in refrigerator by catching bases of glasses between bars of refrigerator rack and leaning tops of glasses against wall. Chill until set but not firm.

WHIP reserved gelatin at high speed of electric mixer until fluffy and thick. Spoon lightly over set gelatin in glasses. Chill upright until set, about 2 hours. Garnish with whipped topping and JELL-O Jigglers, if desired.
MAKES 4 servings

Prep time: 20 minutes
Chill time: 2 hours

Buried Treasure

COOL WHIP Whipped Topping, unthawed
1 package (4-serving size) JELL-O Instant Pudding and Pie Filling, any flavor
2 cups cold milk

SCOOP out small balls of frozen whipped topping, using small ice cream scoop or melon ball cutter. Place 1 in each of 4 dessert dishes. Place in freezer.

PREPARE pudding mix with milk as directed on package. Spoon over whipped topping in dishes. Let stand 5 minutes to set. Chill until ready to serve. *MAKES 4 servings*

Prep time: 10 minutes

Fruity Dip

Fruity Dip

1 package (8 ounces)
   PHILADELPHIA BRAND Cream
   Cheese, softened
1 package (4-serving size) JELL-O
   Brand Gelatin, any flavor
¼ cup milk
   Assorted fruit and cookies*

STIR cream cheese in small bowl until
smooth. Gradually stir in gelatin and
milk until well blended. Chill until ready
to serve. Let stand at room
temperature to soften slightly, if
necessary. Garnish with fruit, if desired.
Serve with fruit and cookies.

MAKES 1½ cups

*We suggest sliced apples or pears,
grapes or strawberries.

Prep time: 5 minutes

Quick Yogurt 'n Pudding

1 cup cold milk
1 container (8 ounces) plain or fruit
   flavor yogurt
1 package (4-serving size) JELL-O
   Instant Pudding and Pie Filling,
   any flavor

MIX milk and yogurt in small bowl. Add
pudding mix. Beat with wire whisk or at
lowest speed of electric mixer until
well blended, 1 to 2 minutes. Pour into
individual serving dishes. Let stand 5
minutes. Chill until ready to serve.

MAKES 4 servings

Prep time: 10 minutes

Banana Cream Pie

Vanilla wafers
Teddy bear cookies
1 large banana, sliced
2½ cups cold milk
1 package (6-serving size) JELL-O
Instant Pudding and Pie Filling,
Banana Cream, Chocolate or
Vanilla Flavor
1 cup thawed COOL WHIP Whipped
Topping (optional)
Gumdrop slices (optional)

COVER bottom of 9-inch pie plate with
vanilla wafers. Arrange additional
vanilla wafers and teddy bear cookies
alternately around sides. Place
banana slices over wafers on bottom
of plate.

POUR milk into small bowl. Add pie
filling mix. Beat with wire whisk until
well blended, 1 to 2 minutes. Pour over
bananas in pie plate. Chill 2 hours.
Garnish with whipped topping,
additional banana slices and
gumdrop slices to resemble tic-tac-
toe game, if desired.

MAKES 8 servings

Prep time: 15 minutes
Chill time: 2 hours

Sailboats

1 package (4-serving size) JELL-O
Brand Gelatin, any flavor
1 can (8 ounces) peach slices,
drained
½ cup banana slices
Paper and wooden picks for sails

Banana Cream Pie

PREPARE gelatin as directed on
package. Chill until slightly thickened.
Reserve 8 peach slices for garnish. Stir
remaining peach and banana slices
into gelatin. Pour into 4 individual
dessert dishes. Chill until firm, about 2
hours.

TOP gelatin with reserved peach
slices. Cut 4 small triangles from paper
to make sails (decorate sails with
crayons, if desired). Insert wooden
picks through sails; place in gelatin.

MAKES 4 servings

Prep time: 20 minutes
Chill time: 2 hours

Rocky Road Pudding

1 package (4-serving size) JELL-O
Instant Pudding and Pie Filling,
Chocolate Flavor
2 cups cold milk
½ cup KRAFT Miniature
Marshmallows
⅓ cup coarsely chopped peanuts
⅓ cup BAKER'S Semi-Sweet Real
Chocolate Chips

PREPARE pudding mix with milk as
directed on package. Let stand 5
minutes. Fold in marshmallows,
peanuts and chocolate chips.

SPOON pudding mixture into individual
dessert dishes. Chill 2 hours. Garnish
with whipped topping and additional
chopped peanuts, if desired.

MAKES 6 servings

Prep time: 10 minutes
Chill time: 2 hours

■ Ice Cream Cone Cakes

1 package (2-layer size) yellow
  cake mix
24 flat-bottom ice cream cones
  Fluffy Pudding Frosting (recipe
  follows)
  Sprinkles (optional)

PREPARE cake mix as directed on
package. Spoon about ¼ cup batter
into each cone. Set cones on baking
sheet. Bake at 350° for 25 minutes.
Cool on rack. Spoon Fluffy Pudding
Frosting over cakes; garnish with
sprinkles, if desired.

MAKES 2 dozen cones

Fluffy Pudding Frosting

1 cup cold milk
1 package (4-serving size) JELL-O
  Instant Pudding and Pie Filling,
  any flavor
¼ cup confectioners sugar
  (optional)
3½ cups (8 ounces) COOL WHIP
  Whipped Topping, thawed

POUR milk into large bowl. Add
pudding mix and sugar. Beat with wire
whisk until well blended, 1 to 2
minutes. Fold in whipped topping.
Spread on cakes immediately.

MAKES about 4 cups

Note: Store frosted cakes in
refrigerator.

Prep time: 15 minutes
Baking time: 25 minutes

■ Chocolate-Cherry Sundaes

1 package (4-serving size) JELL-O
  Brand Gelatin, Cherry Flavor
1 cup boiling water
½ cup cold water
1 cup chocolate ice cream,
  softened
  COOL WHIP Whipped Topping,
  thawed
  Chocolate syrup
  Maraschino cherries (optional)

DISSOLVE gelatin in boiling water.
Measure ½ cup of the gelatin into
small bowl. Add cold water; set aside.
Spoon ice cream into remaining
gelatin, stirring until melted and
smooth. Spoon into individual dessert
dishes. Chill until set but not firm, about
10 minutes.

SPOON reserved gelatin over creamy
layer in dishes. Chill until set, about 1
hour. Top each dessert with dollop of
whipped topping; drizzle with
chocolate syrup. Garnish with cherry, if
desired. *MAKES 6 servings*

Prep time: 15 minutes
Chill time: 1 hour

*Clockwise from top right: Chocolate-
Cherry Sundaes; Ice Cream Cone Cakes;
Gelatin Sundaes (page 128)*

Gelatin Sundaes

1 package (4-serving size) JELL-O
  Brand Gelatin, any flavor
¾ cup boiling water
½ cup cold water
  Ice cubes
1 pint ice cream, any flavor
1 cup thawed COOL WHIP Whipped
  Topping
¼ cup chopped nuts

DISSOLVE gelatin in boiling water. Combine cold water and ice cubes to make 1¼ cups. Add to gelatin, stirring until slightly thickened. Remove any unmelted ice.

SPOON ice cream and gelatin alternately into tall sundae dishes, ending with gelatin and filling to within ½ inch of top of dish. Top with whipped topping and nuts.

MAKES 4 servings

Prep time: 15 minutes

Fluffy Float

1 package (4-serving size) JELL-O
  Brand Gelatin, any flavor
1 cup boiling water
½ cup cold ginger ale or water
1 pint ice cream, any flavor,
  softened

DISSOLVE gelatin in boiling water. Add ginger ale. Spoon in ice cream, stirring until melted and smooth. Chill until slightly thickened. Beat until light and foamy.

POUR gelatin mixture into tall glasses. Chill until firm, about 2 hours. Garnish with whipped topping and Chocolate Curls (see page 22 for directions), if desired. *MAKES 4 servings*

Prep time: 15 minutes
Chill time: 2 hours

Pudding Cones

1 cup cold milk
1 package (4-serving size) JELL-O
  Instant Pudding and Pie Filling,
  any flavor
1 cup thawed COOL WHIP Whipped
  Topping
¼ cup chopped nuts (optional)
4 flat-bottom ice cream cones

POUR milk into small bowl. Add pudding mix. Beat with wire whisk until well blended, 1 to 2 minutes. Fold in whipped topping and nuts. Chill until ready to serve.

SPOON pudding mixture into cones. Garnish with additional whipped topping and nuts, if desired.

MAKES 4 servings

Prep time: 10 minutes

Frozen Fruity Bars and Frozen Pudding Bars

■ Frozen Fruity Bars

    1 package (4-serving size) JELL-O Brand Gelatin, any flavor
    ½ cup sugar
    2 cups boiling water
    2 cups cold water

DISSOLVE gelatin and sugar in boiling water. Add cold water. Pour into pop molds or paper or plastic cups. Freeze until almost firm, about 2 hours. Insert wooden stick or spoon into each cup. Freeze until firm, about 8 hours or overnight.   *MAKES 8 pops*

Prep time: 15 minutes
Freezing time: 10 hours

■ Frozen Pudding Bars

    1 package (4-serving size) JELL-O Instant Pudding and Pie Filling, any flavor
    2 cups cold milk

PREPARE pudding mix with milk as directed on package. Pour into pop molds or paper or plastic cups. Insert wooden stick or spoon into each cup. Freeze until firm, about 5 hours.
    MAKES 6 pops

Prep time: 10 minutes
Freezing time: 5 hours

Merry-Go-Round Cake

- **1 package (6-serving size) JELL-O Instant Pudding and Pie Filling, Vanilla Flavor**
- **1 package (2-layer size) yellow cake mix**
- **4 eggs**
- **1 cup water**
- **¼ cup vegetable oil**
- **⅓ cup BAKER'S Semi-Sweet Real Chocolate Chips, melted**
- **⅔ cup cold milk**
- **Sprinkles (optional)**
- **Paper carousel roof (directions follow)**
- **3 plastic straws**
- **6 animal crackers**

RESERVE ⅓ cup pudding mix. Combine cake mix, remaining pudding mix, eggs, water and oil in large bowl. Beat at low speed of electric mixer just to moisten, scraping sides of bowl often. Beat at medium speed 4 minutes. Pour ½ of the batter into greased and floured 10-inch fluted tube pan. Mix chocolate into remaining batter. Spoon over batter in pan; cut through with spatula in zigzag pattern to marbleize. Bake at 350° for 50 minutes or until cake tester inserted in center comes out clean. Cool in pan 15 minutes. Remove from pan; finish cooling on rack.

BEAT reserved pudding mix and milk in small bowl until smooth. Spoon over top of cake to glaze. Garnish with sprinkles, if desired.

CUT 10- to 12-inch circle from colored paper; scallop edges, if desired. Make 1 slit to center (Diagram 1). Overlap cut edges together to form carousel roof; secure with tape (Diagram 2). Cut straws in half; arrange on cake with animal crackers. Top with roof.
MAKES 12 servings

Prep time: 30 minutes
Baking time: 50 minutes

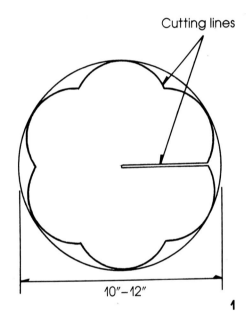

Cutting lines

10″–12″

1

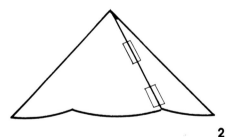

2

Merry-Go-Round Cake

Funny Faces

**1 package (4-serving size) JELL-O
Instant Pudding and Pie Filling,
any flavor**
2 cups cold milk
BAKER'S ANGEL FLAKE Coconut*
Popped popcorn
Assorted candies and nuts
Sprinkles

DECORATE individual dessert dishes
with paper cutouts, if desired.

PREPARE pudding mix with milk as
directed on package. Let stand 5
minutes. Spoon pudding into
decorated dessert dishes. Make faces
on pudding with coconut, popcorn,
candies, nuts and sprinkles. Chill until
ready to serve.   *MAKES 4 servings*

*Coconut may be tinted, if desired
(see page 21 for directions).

Prep time: 20 minutes

Dessert-Wiches

**1 package (4-serving size) JELL-O
Brand Gelatin, any flavor**
1 cup boiling water
¾ cup cold water
**COOL WHIP Whipped Topping,
thawed**
**1 pound cake loaf (about 12
ounces), cut into 24 slices**

DISSOLVE gelatin in boiling water. Add
cold water. Pour gelatin into 9-inch
square pan. Chill until firm, about 3
hours. Cut into 12 rectangles.

SPREAD whipped topping on cake
slices. Place gelatin rectangles on ½
of the cake slices. Top with remaining
cake slices, topping side down. Chill
until ready to serve.
       MAKES 1 dozen dessert-wiches

Prep time: 20 minutes
Chill time: 3 hours

Peanut Butter and Jelly Parfaits

¼ cup peanut butter
2 cups cold milk
**1 package (4-serving size) JELL-O
Instant Pudding and Pie Filling,
Vanilla Flavor**
**1 cup thawed COOL WHIP Whipped
Topping**
½ teaspoon water
**¼ cup raspberry or strawberry jelly
or jam**

STIR peanut butter in small bowl until
smooth. Gradually stir in milk until
smooth. Add pudding mix. Beat with
wire whisk or at lowest speed of
electric mixer until well blended, 1 to 2
minutes. Fold in whipped topping.

STIR water into jelly. Spoon about ¼
cup pudding mixture into each of 5
parfait glasses; top each with about 1
teaspoon jelly. Repeat layers. Garnish
with additional whipped topping, jelly
and chopped peanuts, if desired. Chill
until ready to serve.
       MAKES 5 servings

Prep time: 15 minutes

Funny Faces

Peanut Butter and Jelly Cake-Wiches

½ cup peanut butter
1¼ cups cold milk
1 package (4-serving size) JELL-O Instant Pudding and Pie Filling, Vanilla or Butterscotch Flavor
½ cup jelly or preserves
1 pound cake loaf (about 12 ounces), cut into 16 slices
Chocolate Drizzle (see page 23 for directions)

STIR peanut butter in small bowl until smooth. Gradually stir in milk. Add pudding mix. Beat with wire whisk or at low speed of electric mixer until well blended, 1 to 2 minutes. Chill 15 minutes.

SPREAD jelly thinly over ½ of the cake slices. Spread remaining cake slices with pudding mixture. Prepare sandwiches with cake slices. Chill. Cut into shapes; decorate with Chocolate Drizzle. *MAKES about 1½ dozen cake-wiches*

Prep time: 20 minutes

Clockwise from top left: Chocolate Peanut Butter Cups; Peanut Butter and Jelly Cake-Wiches; Vanilla Peanut Butter Cups

Chocolate Peanut Butter Cups

¾ cup chocolate cookie crumbs
3 tablespoons PARKAY Margarine, melted
½ cup peanut butter
1 cup cold milk
1 package (4-serving size) JELL-O Instant Pudding and Pie Filling, Chocolate Flavor
2 cups thawed COOL WHIP Whipped Topping
Chocolate topping*

LINE 12 muffin cups with paper baking cups. Mix together cookie crumbs and margarine in small bowl. Press about 1 tablespoon crumb mixture onto bottom of each cup.

STIR peanut butter in small bowl until smooth. Gradually stir in milk. Add pudding mix. Beat with wire whisk or at low speed of electric mixer until well blended, 1 to 2 minutes. Fold in whipped topping. Spoon mixture into cups. Freeze 3 hours or overnight. Peel off paper just before serving. Drizzle chocolate topping over each cup. *MAKES 1 dozen cups*

*Use commercial topping that forms hard coating on ice cream.

Vanilla Peanut Butter Cups: Prepare Chocolate Peanut Butter Cups as directed, substituting graham cracker crumbs for chocolate cookie crumbs and vanilla flavor pudding for chocolate flavor pudding. Top each cup with 1 teaspoon strawberry preserves in place of chocolate topping.

Prep time: 10 minutes
Freezing time: 3 hours

Applesauce Yogurt Delight

1 package (4-serving size) JELL-O
    Brand Gelatin, any red flavor
1 cup boiling water
¾ cup chilled unsweetened
    applesauce
¼ teaspoon ground cinnamon
½ cup vanilla yogurt
    Apple slices (optional)
    Mint leaves (optional)

DISSOLVE gelatin in boiling water.
Measure ¾ cup gelatin into small
bowl; add applesauce and
cinnamon. Pour into individual dessert
dishes. Chill until set but not firm. Chill
remaining gelatin until slightly
thickened. Blend in yogurt. Spoon over
set gelatin in dessert dishes. Chill until
set, about 2 hours. Garnish with
additional yogurt, apple slices and
mint leaves, if desired.

MAKES 4 servings

Prep time: 20 minutes
Chill time: 2½ hours

Carousel Pudding Cups

1 package (4-serving size) JELL-O
    Instant Pudding and Pie Filling,
    Vanilla or Chocolate Flavor
2 cups cold milk
    Dinosaur cookies or animal
    crackers
    COOL WHIP Whipped Topping,
    thawed

PREPARE pudding mix with milk as
directed on package. Pour into
individual serving dishes. Chill until
ready to serve. Arrange cookies
around inside rim of each dish. Garnish
with whipped topping.

MAKES 4 servings

Prep time: 10 minutes

Carousel Gelatin Cups

1 package (4-serving size) JELL-O
    Brand Gelatin, any red flavor
    Teddy bear cookies or animal
    crackers
    COOL WHIP Whipped Topping,
    thawed

PREPARE gelatin as directed on
package. Pour into individual serving
dishes. Chill until firm, about 2 hours.
Arrange cookies around inside rim of
each dish. Garnish with whipped
topping.   *MAKES 4 servings*

Prep time: 10 minutes
Chill time: 2 hours

Applesauce Yogurt Delight

Banana Splits

1 package (4-serving size) JELL-O
    Brand Gelatin, any flavor
1 cup boiling water
¾ cup cold water
4 small bananas
1 cup thawed COOL WHIP Whipped
    Topping
½ cup chopped nuts

DISSOLVE gelatin in boiling water. Add cold water. Pour into 9-inch square pan. Chill until firm, about 4 hours.

BREAK gelatin into small flakes with fork, or force through potato ricer or large-meshed strainer. Split bananas lengthwise. Place in oblong dessert dishes; top with gelatin. Garnish with whipped topping; sprinkle with nuts.
MAKES 4 servings

Prep time: 15 minutes
Chill time: 4 hours

Gelatin Snow Cones

1 package (4-serving size) JELL-O
    Brand Gelatin, any flavor
¾ cup boiling water
½ cup cold water
    Ice cubes
½ cup thawed COOL WHIP Whipped
    Topping
4 flat-bottom ice cream cones

DISSOLVE gelatin in boiling water. Combine cold water and ice cubes to make 1¼ cups. Add to gelatin, stirring until slightly thickened. Remove any unmelted ice. Chill until firm, about 3 hours.

BREAK gelatin into small flakes with fork, or force through potato ricer or large-meshed strainer. Fold in whipped topping. Spoon or scoop into cones.
MAKES 4 servings

Prep time: 15 minutes
Chill time: 3 hours

Pudding "Pizza"

1 package (17 ounces) refrigerated
    cookie dough
1¼ cups cold milk
1 package (4-serving size) JELL-O
    Instant Pudding and Pie Filling,
    any flavor
1 cup thawed COOL WHIP Whipped
    Topping
    Assorted fruit and candies

CUT cookie dough into ¼-inch slices. Place in ungreased 12-inch pizza pan; press evenly together onto bottom and up sides to form crust. Bake at 350° for 15 minutes or until golden. Cool on rack.

POUR milk into small bowl. Add pudding mix. Beat with wire whisk until well blended, 1 to 2 minutes. Let stand 5 minutes. Fold in whipped topping. Spread evenly over crust. Arrange fruit and candies on pudding. Chill until ready to serve. Cut "pizza" into slices.
MAKES 12 servings

Prep time: 20 minutes
Baking time: 15 minutes

▪ Bunny in a Cloud

**2 cups thawed COOL WHIP
    Whipped Topping**
**1 package (4-serving size) JELL-O
    Instant Pudding and Pie Filling,
    any flavor**
2 cups cold milk
**2 tablespoons BAKER'S Semi-Sweet
    Real Chocolate Chips**
6 Bunny Faces (directions follow)

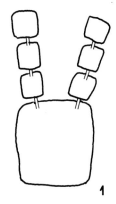

1

DIVIDE whipped topping among 6 individual dessert dishes, spooning about ⅓ cup whipped topping into each dish. With back of spoon, make depression in center; spread topping up sides of dish.

PREPARE pudding mix with milk as directed on package. Fold in chocolate chips. Spoon pudding mixture into dishes. Chill.

PREPARE Bunny Faces. Place in pudding just before serving.

MAKES 6 servings

Bunny Faces: For each face, insert each of 2 wooden picks into 3 miniature marshmallows. Attach to large marshmallow to resemble ears (Diagram 1). Make face on large marshmallow using cut pieces of gumdrops or decorating gel. Attach face to large marshmallow turned sideways for body, using additional wooden pick (Diagram 2).

2

Prep time: 20 minutes

■ Fruity Ice Cream "Sodas"

1 package (4-serving size) JELL-O Brand Gelatin, any flavor
1 cup boiling water
1 cup cold club soda
¼ cup cold water
1 cup vanilla ice cream

DISSOLVE gelatin in boiling water. Add club soda and cold water. Chill until slightly thickened. Measure 1 cup gelatin mixture into small bowl; set aside.

PLACE small scoop of ice cream in each of 3 (12-ounce) soda glasses. Fill glasses ⅔ full with thickened gelatin. Beat reserved gelatin until light and fluffy; spoon over gelatin in glasses. Chill until firm, about 2 hours. Top with whipped topping and mint leaves, if desired.   *MAKES 3 servings*

Prep time: 15 minutes
Chill time: 2½ hours

■ Pinstripe Parfaits

1 package (4-serving size) JELL-O Brand Gelatin, Cherry, Strawberry or Raspberry Flavor
1 cup boiling water
1 cup cold water
  Half and half or milk

DISSOLVE gelatin in boiling water. Add cold water. Pour into dessert glasses, filling each to about 1 inch from top. Chill until firm, about 3 hours.

POUR ½ inch of half and half into each glass. Using drinking straw, make deep tunnels at intervals around outside and through center of gelatin, allowing half and half to settle into tunnels.   *MAKES 4 servings*

Prep time: 10 minutes
Chill time: 3 hours

■ Jack-O'-Lantern Pie

1 package (4-serving size) JELL-O Brand Gelatin, Orange Flavor
1 cup boiling water
1 pint vanilla ice cream, softened
1 packaged chocolate crumb crust
  COOL WHIP Whipped Topping, thawed (optional)
  Candy corn (optional)
  Black licorice, cut into 1-inch pieces (optional)

DISSOLVE gelatin in boiling water. Spoon in ice cream, stirring until melted and smooth. Chill until slightly thickened, about 10 minutes.

POUR gelatin mixture into crust. Chill until firm, about 2 hours. Garnish with whipped topping. Make jack-o'-lantern face on pie with candy corn and licorice, if desired.
          MAKES 8 servings

Prep time: 15 minutes
Chill time: 2 hours

Top: Jack-O'-Lantern Pie; bottom: Jell-O Apple Jigglers (page 142); Jell-O Jigglers (page 143)

FUN WITH JELL-O JIGGLERS

JELL-O Apple Jigglers
Gelatin Snacks

2½ cups boiling water or boiling fruit
    juice
  4 packages (4-serving size each) or
    2 packages (8-serving size
    each) JELL-O Brand Gelatin, any
    flavor
1½ cups chopped peeled apples

ADD boiling water to gelatin. Dissolve
completely; cool slightly. Pour ½ of the
gelatin into blender. Add ½ of the
apples; cover. Blend at high speed 1
minute. Pour into 13×9-inch pan.
Repeat with remaining gelatin and
apples. Pour into pan. Chill until firm,
about 3 hours.

DIP pan in warm water about 15
seconds for easy removal. Use cookie
cutters to cut gelatin mixture into
decorative shapes (hearts for
Valentine's Day, pumpkins for
Halloween, stars for sports parties,
etc.). Remove from pan. Cut
remaining gelatin into cubes.
   MAKES about 3 dozen JELL-O Jigglers

JELL-O "Pumpkin" Jigglers: Cut
gelatin mixture into pumpkin shapes
with cookie cutter. Decorate with
candies to make jack-o'-lantern
faces, if desired.

Prep time: 15 minutes
Chill time: 3 hours

JELL-O Tropical Jigglers
Gelatin Snacks

2½ cups boiling water or boiling fruit
    juice
  4 packages (4-serving size each) or
    2 packages (8-serving size
    each) JELL-O Brand Gelatin,
    Strawberry-Banana or Orange
    Flavor
  1 can (8 ounces) crushed
    pineapple in juice, undrained

ADD boiling water to gelatin. Dissolve
completely. Stir in pineapple. Pour into
13×9-inch pan. Chill until firm, about 3
hours.

DIP pan in warm water about 15
seconds for easy removal. Use cookie
cutters to cut decorative shapes in
gelatin; remove from pan. Cut
remaining gelatin into cubes.
   MAKES about 3 dozen JELL-O Jigglers

Prep time: 10 minutes
Chill time: 3 hours

JELL-O Jigglers
Gelatin Snacks

2½ cups boiling water or boiling fruit juice
4 packages (4-serving size each) or 2 packages (8-serving size each) JELL-O Brand Gelatin, any flavor

ADD boiling water to gelatin. Dissolve completely. Pour into 13×9-inch pan. Chill until firm, about 3 hours.

DIP pan in warm water about 15 seconds for easy removal. Use cookie cutters to cut decorative shapes in gelatin (hearts for Valentine's Day, pumpkins for Halloween, stars for sports parties, etc.). Remove JELL-O Jigglers from pan. Cut remaining gelatin into cubes.

MAKES about 3 dozen JELL-O Jigglers

Notes: For thicker Jigglers, use 8-or 9-inch square pan.

To use ice cube trays or Jiggler molds, pour dissolved gelatin into 2 or 3 ice cube trays. Chill until firm, about 2 hours. To remove, dip trays in warm water about 15 seconds. Moisten tips of fingers; gently pull Jigglers from edges and remove from trays.

Prep time: 10 minutes
Chill time: 3 hours

JELL-O Jiggler Surprises
Gelatin Snacks

2½ cups boiling water or boiling fruit
    juice
  4 packages (4-serving size each) or
    2 packages (8-serving size
    each) JELL-O Brand Gelatin, any
    flavor
  Banana slices
  Strawberry slices
  **Canned pineapple slices, cut into
    bite-size pieces**

ADD boiling water to gelatin. Dissolve
completely. Pour into 13×9-inch pan.
Arrange fruit in gelatin so that when
cut into decorative shapes, each will
contain 1 piece of fruit. Chill until firm,
about 3 hours.

DIP pan in warm water about 15
seconds for easy removal. Use cookie
cutters to cut gelatin into decorative
shapes; remove JELL-O Jigglers from
pan. Cut remaining gelatin into cubes.
   MAKES about 3 dozen JELL-O Jigglers

Prep time: 10 minutes
Chill time: 3 hours

JELL-O Fruity Yogurt Jigglers
Gelatin Snacks

2½ cups boiling water or boiling fruit
    juice
  4 packages (4-serving size each) or
    2 packages (8-serving size
    each) JELL-O Brand Gelatin, any
    flavor
  2 containers (8 ounces each)
    vanilla or fruit flavor yogurt

ADD boiling water to gelatin. Dissolve
completely. Cool to room
temperature. Stir in yogurt with wire
whisk until well blended. Pour into
13×9-inch pan. Chill until firm, about
3 hours.

DIP pan in warm water about 15
seconds for easy removal. Use cookie
cutters to cut decorative shapes in
gelatin; remove from pan. Cut
remaining gelatin into cubes.
   MAKES about 3 dozen JELL-O Jigglers

Prep time: 10 minutes
Chill time: 3 hours

*JELL-O Jigglers (page 143); JELL-O Jiggler
Surprises; JELL-O Fruity Yogurt Jigglers;
JELL-O Tropical Jigglers (page 142);
JELL-O Creamy Jigglers (page 146); and
JELL-O Vegetable Jigglers (page 200)*

JELL-O Creamy Jigglers
Gelatin Snacks

2½ cups boiling water or boiling fruit
    juice
  4 packages (4-serving size each) or
    2 packages (8-serving size
    each) JELL-O Brand Gelatin, any
    flavor
  1 cup cold milk
  1 package (4-serving size) JELL-O
    Instant Pudding and Pie Filling,
    Vanilla Flavor

ADD boiling water to gelatin. Dissolve
completely; cool to room
temperature.

POUR milk into small bowl. Add
pudding mix. Beat with wire whisk until
well blended, 1 to 2 minutes. Quickly
pour into gelatin. Stir with wire whisk
until well blended. Pour into 13×9-inch
pan. Chill until firm, about 3 hours.

DIP pan into warm water about 15
seconds for easy removal. Use cookie
cutters to cut decorative shapes
(umbrellas for showers, etc.). Cut
remaining gelatin into cubes.
MAKES about 3 dozen JELL-O Jigglers

Notes: For thicker JELL-O Jigglers, use
8- or 9-inch square pan.

To use ice cube trays or JELL-O Jiggler
molds, pour dissolved gelatin mixture
into 2 or 3 ice cube trays. Chill until
firm, about 2 hours. To remove JELL-O
Jigglers, dip trays in warm water about
15 seconds. Moisten tips of fingers and
gently pull from edges.

Prep time: 15 minutes
Chill time: 3 hours

Circa 1925

THE CLASSICS

■ Under-the-Sea Salad

1 can (16 ounces) pear halves in syrup, undrained
1 package (4-serving size) JELL-O Brand Gelatin, Lime Flavor
1 cup boiling water
¼ cup cold water
1 tablespoon lemon juice
1 package (8 ounces) PHILADELPHIA BRAND Cream Cheese, softened
⅛ teaspoon ground ginger
Salad greens (optional)
Seedless red grapes (optional)

DRAIN pears, reserving ½ cup syrup. Dice pears; set aside. Dissolve gelatin in boiling water. Add reserved syrup, cold water and lemon juice. Measure 1¼ cups gelatin into 8×4-inch loaf pan. Chill until set but not firm. Place cream cheese in blender; cover. Blend at low speed until smooth and creamy. Very slowly add remaining gelatin and ginger. Blend at low speed until smooth, about 15 seconds. Chill until thickened. Fold in pears. Spoon over gelatin in pan. Chill until firm, about 2 hours. Unmold. Garnish with crisp salad greens, additional pears and grapes, if desired.

MAKES 8 servings

Light Under-the-Sea Salad: Prepare Under-the-Sea Salad as directed, using pear halves in juice or light syrup, JELL-O Brand Sugar Free Gelatin and PHILADELPHIA BRAND LIGHT Neufchatel Cheese.

Prep time: 20 minutes
Chill time: 3 hours

Under-the-Sea Salad

■ Sunset Yogurt Salad

2 packages (4-serving size each) or
    1 package (8-serving size)
    JELL-O Brand Gelatin, Orange or
    Lemon Flavor
2 cups boiling water
1 container (8 ounces) plain or
    pineapple-orange yogurt
¼ cup cold water
1 can (8 ounces) crushed
    pineapple in juice, undrained
1 cup shredded carrots
    Carrot Curls (see page 24 for
    directions) (optional)
    Curly leaf lettuce (optional)
    Canned pineapple slices,
    drained (optional)

DISSOLVE gelatin in boiling water. Measure 1 cup gelatin into small bowl; chill until slightly thickened. Stir in yogurt. Pour into serving bowl. Chill until set but not firm. Stir cold water into remaining gelatin. Add pineapple and carrots. Chill until slightly thickened. Spoon over gelatin-yogurt mixture in bowl.

CHILL gelatin until firm, about 4 hours. Garnish with Carrot Curls, lettuce leaves and pineapple slices, if desired.
MAKES 10 servings

Prep time: 20 minutes
Chill time: 5 hours

■ Gazpacho Salad

1 cup diced tomatoes
½ cup diced peeled cucumbers
¼ cup diced green peppers
2 tablespoons diced red peppers
2 tablespoons thinly sliced
    scallions
2 tablespoons vinegar
¼ teaspoon ground black pepper
⅛ teaspoon garlic powder
    (optional)
1 package (4-serving size) JELL-O
    Brand Gelatin, Lemon Flavor
1½ cups tomato juice

COMBINE tomato, cucumber, green pepper, red pepper, scallions, vinegar, ground black pepper and garlic powder in medium bowl; mix well.

DISSOLVE gelatin in boiling tomato juice. Chill until thickened. Fold in vegetable mixture.

POUR gelatin mixture into 3-cup mold or serving bowl. Chill until firm, about 3 hours. Unmold. Garnish with tomato and cucumber slices, if desired.
MAKES 6 servings

Prep time: 20 minutes
Chill time: 3½ hours

Imperial Salad

1 can (8 ounces) crushed or chunk pineapple in juice, undrained
1 package (4-serving size) JELL-O Brand Gelatin, Lemon or Lime Flavor
1 cup boiling water
1 to 2 tablespoons vinegar
1 cup diced cucumber
¼ cup finely chopped red pepper

DRAIN pineapple, reserving juice. Add water to juice to make ¾ cup.

DISSOLVE gelatin in boiling water. Add measured liquid and vinegar. Chill until slightly thickened. Fold in pineapple, cucumber and red pepper.

POUR gelatin mixture into 3-cup mold or individual molds. Chill until firm, about 3 hours. Unmold. Garnish with crisp salad greens and cucumber slices, if desired.   *MAKES 6 servings*

Prep time: 20 minutes
Chill time: 3½ hours

Three Pepper Salad

2 packages (4-serving size each) or 1 package (8-serving size) JELL-O Brand Gelatin, Lemon Flavor
2 cups boiling water
1½ cups cold water
2 tablespoons lemon juice
2 cups chopped red, green and/or yellow peppers
2 tablespoons sliced scallions
Salsa Dressing (recipe follows) (optional)

DISSOLVE gelatin in boiling water. Stir in cold water and lemon juice. Chill until thickened. Fold in peppers and scallions. Pour gelatin mixture into 5-cup mold. Chill until firm, about 4 hours. Unmold. Cut into slices; serve with Salsa Dressing, if desired.
MAKES 10 servings

Salsa Dressing

½ cup MIRACLE WHIP Salad Dressing
½ cup sour cream
½ cup prepared salsa

MIX together ingredients until well blended. Chill.   *MAKES 1½ cups*

Garden Salad: Prepare Three Pepper Salad as directed, substituting 1 cup shredded carrots, 1 cup shredded zucchini, ½ cup chopped red pepper and 2 tablespoons finely chopped onion for the peppers and scallions.

Prep time: 20 minutes
Chill time: 4½ hours

Three Pepper Salad

■ Vegetable Trio

2 packages (4-serving size each) or
  1 package (8-serving size)
  JELL-O Brand Gelatin, Lemon
  Flavor
½ teaspoon salt
2 cups boiling water
1½ cups cold water
3 tablespoons vinegar
1½ cups shredded carrots
½ cup mayonnaise
1 cup shredded zucchini
¼ cup sliced scallions
  Carrot Curls (see page 24 for
    directions) (optional)
  Scallion Brushes (see page 24 for
    directions) (optional)
  Celery leaves (optional)

DISSOLVE gelatin and salt in boiling water. Add cold water and vinegar. Measure 1⅓ cups gelatin into small bowl. Place bowl in larger bowl of ice and water. Stir until slightly thickened. Fold in carrots. Pour into 6-cup mold or 9×5-inch loaf pan. Chill until set but not firm. Measure 1 cup of the remaining gelatin into small bowl; stir in mayonnaise. Chill over ice until thickened. Spoon over gelatin mixture in mold. Chill until set but not firm.

CHILL remaining gelatin over ice until slightly thickened. Fold in zucchini and scallions. Spoon over creamy layer in mold. Chill until firm, about 3 hours. Unmold. Garnish with Carrot Curls, Scallion Brushes and celery leaves, if desired.   *MAKES 12 servings*

Prep time: 30 minutes
Chill time: 4 hours

Vegetable Trio

■ Avocado Barbecue Salad

2 packages (4-serving size each) or
  1 package (8-serving size)
  JELL-O Brand Gelatin, Lemon
  Flavor
½ teaspoon salt
2 cups boiling water
1 can (15 ounces) tomato sauce
2 tablespoons vinegar
½ teaspoon hot pepper sauce
2 cups chopped avocado
½ cup finely chopped celery
¼ cup sliced scallions

DISSOLVE gelatin and salt in boiling water. Stir in tomato sauce, vinegar and hot pepper sauce. Chill until thickened. Fold in avocado, celery and scallions. Pour into 5-cup mold. Chill until firm, about 4 hours. Unmold. Garnish as desired.
          MAKES 10 servings

Prep time: 20 minutes
Chill time: 4½ hours

■ Shimmering Shrimp Mold

2 packages (4-serving size each) or
    1 package (8-serving size)
    JELL-O Brand Gelatin, Lemon or
    Lime Flavor
½ teaspoon salt
2 cups boiling water
1 cup cold water
2 tablespoons vinegar
1 pound cooked cleaned small
    shrimp (about 2 cups)
½ cup sliced celery
¼ cup chopped red pepper
1 cup (½ pint) sour cream or plain
    yogurt
1 tablespoon chopped parsley
1 tablespoon chopped onion
1 teaspoon curry powder
    (optional)
    Salad greens
    Citrus Twist (see page 17 for
        directions) (optional)
    Watercress (optional)

DISSOLVE gelatin and salt in boiling water. Add cold water and vinegar. Chill until thickened.

MEASURE 1½ cups gelatin into medium bowl. Fold in 1½ cups of the shrimp, celery and red pepper. Spoon into 6-cup ring mold. Chill until set but not firm.

STIR sour cream, parsley, onion and curry into remaining gelatin. Spoon over shrimp layer in mold. Chill until firm, about 4 hours. Unmold. Serve with crisp salad greens and remaining shrimp. Garnish with Citrus Twist and watercress, if desired.

MAKES 6 servings

Prep time: 30 minutes
Chill time: 5 hours

■ Oriental Salad

1 package (4-serving size) JELL-O
    Brand Gelatin, Lemon or
    Orange Flavor
¾ cup boiling water
½ cup cold water
    Ice cubes
1 tablespoon soy sauce
1 tablespoon lemon juice
½ cup shredded carrots
½ cup sliced celery
½ cup drained canned bean
    sprouts
¼ cup chopped water chestnuts
2 tablespoons sliced scallions

DISSOLVE gelatin in boiling water. Combine cold water and ice cubes to make 1 cup. Add to gelatin. Stir until slightly thickened. Remove any unmelted ice. Stir in soy sauce and lemon juice. Fold in carrots, celery, bean sprouts, water chestnuts and scallions. Spoon into serving bowl or individual dishes. Chill until set, at least 30 minutes.   *MAKES 4 to 6 servings*

Prep time: 20 minutes
Chill time: 30 minutes

Shimmering Shrimp Mold

■ Seafood Mousse

1 package (4-serving size) JELL-O Brand Gelatin, Lemon Flavor
¼ teaspoon salt
¾ cup boiling water
1 cup (½ pint) sour cream
½ cup MIRACLE WHIP Salad Dressing
2 tablespoons horseradish
2 tablespoons lemon juice
2 tablespoons grated onion
2 cups seafood*
2 tablespoons chopped fresh dill**
Assorted crackers and fresh vegetables
Citrus Curls (see page 18 for directions) (optional)

DISSOLVE gelatin and salt in boiling water. Stir in sour cream, salad dressing, horseradish, lemon juice and onion. Chill until slightly thickened. Fold in seafood and dill.

SPOON gelatin mixture into 4-cup mold. Chill until firm, about 3 hours. Unmold. Serve with crackers and vegetables. Garnish with additional dill and Citrus Curls, if desired.

MAKES 4 cups

*We suggest 1 can (15 or 16 ounces) red salmon, drained and flaked, or 2 cans (6 ounces each) crab meat, drained and flaked, or 2 cups cooked cleaned shrimp, chopped, or 2 cups chopped imitation crab meat.

**1½ teaspoons dried dillweed may be substituted for fresh dill.

Prep time: 20 minutes
Chill time: 3½ hours

■ Chef's Salad Mold

2 packages (4-serving size each) or 1 package (8-serving size) JELL-O Brand Gelatin, Lemon or Lime Flavor
1 teaspoon salt
2 cups boiling water
1 cup cold water
3 tablespoons vinegar
⅛ teaspoon hot pepper sauce
¾ cup diced Swiss and/or processed American cheese
¾ cup diced tomato
½ cup diced cooked ham
½ cup shredded lettuce
½ cup diced green pepper
½ cup diced cooked turkey
3 tablespoons thinly sliced scallions

DISSOLVE gelatin and salt in boiling water. Add cold water, vinegar and hot pepper sauce. Chill until thickened. Fold in remaining ingredients.

POUR gelatin mixture into 5-cup mold. Chill until firm, about 6 hours or overnight. Unmold. Garnish with crisp salad greens and tomato wedges, if desired. *MAKES 4 to 6 servings*

Prep time: 30 minutes
Chill time: 6½ hours

Seafood Mousse

Tomato Dill Salad

1 package (4-serving size) JELL-O Brand Gelatin, Lemon Flavor
1 cup boiling water
¾ cup tomato juice
1 tablespoon chopped fresh dill*
1 teaspoon lemon juice
1 teaspoon Worcestershire sauce
½ cup chopped celery

DISSOLVE gelatin in boiling water. Add tomato juice, dill, lemon juice and Worcestershire sauce. Chill until thickened. Fold in celery.

SPOON gelatin mixture into 2-cup mold or individual molds. Chill until firm, about 3 hours. Unmold. Garnish with crisp salad greens, if desired.
MAKES 4 servings

*½ teaspoon dried dillweed may be substituted for 1 tablespoon fresh dill.

Prep time: 15 minutes
Chill time: 3½ hours

Chicken and Grape Salad

1 package (4-serving size) JELL-O Brand Gelatin, Lemon or Lime Flavor
½ teaspoon salt
1 cup boiling water
¼ teaspoon tarragon leaves
¾ cup cold water
1 tablespoon lemon juice
1 cup diced cooked chicken or turkey
1 cup green or red seedless grapes, halved
½ cup diced celery

DISSOLVE gelatin and salt in boiling water; add tarragon. Add cold water and lemon juice. Chill until thickened. Fold in chicken, grapes and celery.

POUR gelatin mixture into 4-cup mold or individual molds. Chill until firm, about 4 hours. Unmold. Garnish with crisp salad greens and additional grapes, if desired.
MAKES 4 servings

Prep time: 20 minutes
Chill time: 4½ hours

Watergate Salad

1 package (4-serving size) JELL-O Instant Pudding and Pie Filling, Pistachio Flavor
1 can (20 ounces) crushed pineapple in syrup, undrained
1 cup KRAFT Miniature Marshmallows
½ cup chopped nuts
1¾ cups (4 ounces) COOL WHIP Whipped Topping, thawed

COMBINE pudding mix, pineapple, marshmallows and nuts in large bowl; mix well. Fold in whipped topping. Chill until ready to serve. Garnish with additional whipped topping and fresh fruit, if desired.   *MAKES 8 servings*

Prep time: 15 minutes

■ Ribbon Squares

1 package (4-serving size) JELL-O
    Brand Gelatin, Lemon Flavor
1 package (4-serving size) JELL-O
    Brand Gelatin, Cherry,
    Raspberry or Strawberry Flavor
1 package (4-serving size) JELL-O
    Brand Gelatin, Lime Flavor
3 cups boiling water
1 package (8 ounces)
    PHILADELPHIA BRAND Cream
    Cheese, softened
1 can (8¼ ounces) crushed
    pineapple in syrup, undrained
1 cup thawed COOL WHIP Whipped
    Topping
½ cup MIRACLE WHIP Salad Dressing
1½ cups cold water
    Canned pineapple slices,
      drained (optional)
    Celery leaves (optional)

DISSOLVE each flavor of gelatin in separate bowls, using 1 cup of the boiling water for each.

BLEND lemon gelatin into cream cheese, beating until smooth. Add pineapple with syrup. Chill until slightly thickened. Stir in whipped topping and salad dressing. Chill until thickened. Stir ¾ cup of the cold water into cherry gelatin; pour into 9-inch square pan. Chill until set but not firm. Stir remaining ¾ cup cold water into lime gelatin; chill until slightly thickened. Spoon lemon gelatin mixture over cherry gelatin layer in pan. Chill until set but not firm. Top with lime gelatin. Chill until firm, about 4 hours or overnight. Unmold; cut into squares. Garnish with pineapple slices and celery leaves, if desired. *MAKES 12 servings*

Prep time: 1 hour
Chill time: 6 hours

DESSERTS

■ Ambrosia

1 package (4-serving size) JELL-O
    Brand Gelatin, any flavor
¾ cup boiling water
½ cup cold water
    Ice cubes
1 cup (½ pint) sour cream
1 can (11 ounces) mandarin
    orange sections, drained
1 can (8 ounces) crushed
    pineapple, drained
1 cup KRAFT Miniature
    Marshmallows
¼ cup BAKER'S ANGEL FLAKE
    Coconut

DISSOLVE gelatin in boiling water. Combine cold water and ice cubes to make 1¼ cups. Add to gelatin, stirring until slightly thickened. Remove any unmelted ice. Stir in sour cream until smooth. Fold in oranges, pineapple, marshmallows and coconut. Pour into serving bowl or individual dessert glasses. Chill until set, about 2 hours. Garnish with additional fruit and mint leaves, if desired. *MAKES 8 servings*

Note: Some of the fruit may be reserved for garnish, if desired.

Prep time: 15 minutes
Chill time: 2 hours

■ Rainbow Ribbon

5 packages (4-serving size each)
    JELL-O Brand Gelatin, any
    5 flavors
6¼ cups boiling water
1 cup (½ pint) sour cream or plain
    or vanilla yogurt

DISSOLVE 1 package gelatin in 1¼ cups of the boiling water. Pour ¾ cup of the gelatin into 6-cup ring mold. Chill until set but not firm, about 15 minutes. Chill remaining gelatin in bowl until slightly thickened; gradually blend in 3 tablespoons of the sour cream. Spoon over gelatin in mold. Chill until set but not firm, about 15 minutes.

REPEAT with remaining gelatin flavors, chilling dissolved gelatin before measuring. Chill until firm, about 2 hours. Unmold.

MAKES 12 servings

Prep time: 1 hour
Chill time: 4 hours

■ Strawberries Romanoff

1 pint strawberries
2 tablespoons sugar
2 packages (4-serving size each) or
    1 package (8-serving size)
    JELL-O Brand Gelatin,
    Strawberry Flavor
2 cups boiling water
2 tablespoons brandy*
1 tablespoon orange liqueur*
1¾ cups (4 ounces) COOL WHIP
    Whipped Topping, thawed

SLICE strawberries, reserving a few whole strawberries for garnish, if desired. Add sugar to sliced strawberries. Let stand 15 minutes; drain, reserving syrup. Add cold water to syrup to make 1 cup.

DISSOLVE gelatin in boiling water. Measure ¾ cup gelatin into medium bowl; add brandy, liqueur and ½ cup of the measured liquid. Chill until slightly thickened. Fold in whipped topping. Pour into 6-cup mold. Chill until set but not firm. Stir remaining ½ cup liquid into remaining gelatin. Chill until slightly thickened. Fold in sliced strawberries. Spoon over creamy layer in mold. Chill until firm, about 4 hours. Unmold. Garnish with reserved strawberries, if desired.

MAKES 12 servings

*½ teaspoon brandy extract and 3 tablespoons orange juice may be substituted for brandy and orange liqueur.

Prep time: 30 minutes
Chill time: 4 hours

■ Charlotte Russe

2 packages (4-serving size each) or
    1 package (8-serving size)
    JELL-O Brand Gelatin, any red
    flavor
2 cups boiling water
1 quart vanilla ice cream, softened
12 ladyfingers, split
    COOL WHIP Whipped Topping,
    thawed (optional)
    Fresh raspberries (optional)
    Mint leaves (optional)

DISSOLVE gelatin in boiling water. Spoon in ice cream, stirring until melted and smooth. Chill until thickened.

TRIM about 1 inch off one end of each ladyfinger; reserve trimmed ends for snacking or other use. Place ladyfingers, cut ends down, around sides of 8-inch springform pan. Spoon gelatin mixture into pan. Chill until firm, about 3 hours. Remove sides of pan. Garnish with whipped topping, raspberries and mint leaves, if desired.

MAKES 10 servings

Prep time: 20 minutes
Chill time: 3 hours

Charlotte Russe

■ Crown Jewel Dessert

1 package (4-serving size) JELL-O
  Brand Gelatin, Lime Flavor
1 package (4-serving size) JELL-O
  Brand Gelatin, Orange Flavor
2 packages (4-serving size each)
  JELL-O Brand Gelatin,
  Strawberry Flavor
4 cups boiling water
2 cups cold water
1¾ cups (4 ounces) COOL WHIP
  Whipped Topping, thawed

PREPARE lime, orange and 1 package
of the strawberry gelatin separately,
using 1 cup boiling water and ½ cup
cold water for each. Pour each flavor
into separate 8-inch square pans. Chill
until firm, about 3 hours. Cut into
½-inch cubes. Measure 1½ cups of
each flavor. (Use remaining cubes for
snacking or to prepare Rainbow in a
Cloud; see page 44 for recipe.)

DISSOLVE remaining package of
strawberry gelatin in remaining 1 cup
boiling water. Stir in remaining ½ cup
cold water. Chill until slightly
thickened. Fold in whipped topping,
then measured gelatin cubes. Pour
into 9x5-inch loaf pan. Chill until firm,
about 6 hours or overnight. Unmold.
Garnish with additional whipped
topping and gelatin cubes, if desired.
MAKES 16 servings

Prep time: 1 hour
Chill time: 10 hours

■ Cherries Supreme

1 can (16 ounces) pitted dark sweet
  cherries, undrained
1 package (4-serving size) JELL-O
  Brand Gelatin, any red flavor
1 cup boiling water
1 can (11 ounces) mandarin
  orange sections, drained
1 cup thawed COOL WHIP Whipped
  Topping
¼ cup chopped almonds, toasted
  (see page 19 for directions)

DRAIN cherries, reserving ¾ cup of the
syrup. Dissolve gelatin in boiling water.
Add reserved syrup. Chill until
thickened. Fold in cherries and orange
sections. Pour into 4-cup mold or
individual molds. Chill until firm, about
4 hours.

COMBINE whipped topping and
toasted almonds. Unmold gelatin.
Serve with whipped topping mixture.
MAKES 8 servings

Prep time: 15 minutes
Chill time: 4 hours

Crown Jewel Dessert

■ Glazed Fruit Pie

Tart Shell (recipe follows)*
1½ cups cold half and half or milk
1 package (4-serving size) JELL-O Instant Pudding and Pie Filling, French Vanilla or Vanilla Flavor
1 package (4-serving size) JELL-O Brand Gelatin, Lemon, Peach or Orange Flavor or any red flavor
1 cup boiling water
½ cup cold water
2 cups (about) fresh or drained canned fruit**

PREPARE Tart Shell as directed.

POUR half and half into small bowl. Add pie filling mix. Beat with wire whisk until well blended, 1 to 2 minutes. Pour into tart shell. Chill 1 hour.

DISSOLVE gelatin in boiling water. Add cold water. Chill until thickened. Pour about 1 cup of the gelatin over pie filling. Arrange fruit on gelatin in tart shell; spoon remaining gelatin over fruit. Chill until set, about 2 hours. Remove sides of tart pan before serving.   *MAKES 10 servings*

*½ (15-ounce) package refrigerated pie crust (1 crust), baked and cooled as directed on package, may be substituted for prepared Tart Shell.

**We suggest any variety of berries, mandarin orange sections, halved seedless grapes or sliced bananas, peaches or plums.

Tart Shell

1 package (10 ounces) pie crust mix
1 egg
Cold water

PREHEAT oven to 425°. Mix pie crust mix with egg. Add just enough cold water to form dough, about 1 to 2 tablespoons. On lightly floured surface, roll out pastry to 12-inch round. Fit loosely into 11-inch tart pan with removable bottom. Fold pastry under to form standing rim; flute edges. Bake 20 minutes or until golden. Cool on rack.

Prep time: 25 minutes
Baking time: 20 minutes
Chill time: 3 hours

Glazed Fruit Pie

■ Pink Pastel Party Pie

1 package (10 ounces) BIRDS EYE Quick Thaw Raspberries or Strawberries, thawed
1 package (4-serving size) JELL-O Brand Gelatin, any red flavor
1 pint vanilla ice cream, softened
1 packaged graham cracker crumb crust
Strawberry Fan (see page 19 for directions) (optional)

DRAIN fruit, reserving syrup. Add water to syrup to make 1 cup. Bring liquid to boil. Dissolve gelatin in boiling liquid. Spoon in ice cream, stirring until melted and smooth. Chill until thickened, about 20 minutes.

FOLD raspberries into gelatin mixture. Pour into crust. Chill until firm, about 2 hours. Garnish with Strawberry Fan, if desired. *MAKES 8 servings*

Prep time: 15 minutes
Chill time: 2 hours

■ Lemon Chiffon Pie

3 egg yolks, slightly beaten
1½ cups water
½ cup sugar
1 package (4-serving size) JELL-O Brand Gelatin, Lemon Flavor
1½ teaspoons grated lemon rind
3 tablespoons lemon juice
3 egg whites
1 baked 9-inch pie shell or graham cracker crumb crust, cooled
Citrus Zest Strips (see page 17 for directions) (optional)

COMBINE egg yolks and 1 cup of the water in small saucepan; add ¼ cup of the sugar. Cook and stir over low heat until slightly thickened. Remove from heat. Add gelatin; stir until dissolved. Add remaining ½ cup water, lemon rind and juice. Chill until slightly thickened.

BEAT egg whites until foamy. Gradually beat in remaining ¼ cup sugar; continue beating until stiff peaks form. Fold in thickened gelatin until well blended. Chill until mixture will mound. Spoon into pie shell. Chill until firm, about 4 hours. Garnish with Citrus Zest Strips, if desired. *MAKES 8 servings*

NOTE: USE ONLY CLEAN EGGS WITH NO CRACKS IN SHELLS.

Prep time: 30 minutes
Chill time: 4½ hours

Top to bottom: Pink Pastel Party Pie; Lemon Chiffon Pie; Key Lime Pie (page 172)

■ Key Lime Pie

2 packages (4-serving size each) or
    1 package (8-serving size)
    JELL-O Brand Gelatin, Lime
    Flavor
2 cups boiling water
2 teaspoons grated lime rind
¼ cup lime juice
1 pint vanilla ice cream, softened
1 packaged graham cracker
    crumb crust
    COOL WHIP Whipped Topping,
    thawed (optional)

DISSOLVE gelatin in boiling water. Add lime rind and juice. Spoon in ice cream, stirring until melted and smooth. Chill until mixture will mound.

SPOON gelatin mixture into crust. Chill until firm, about 2 hours. Garnish with whipped topping, if desired.

MAKES 8 servings

Prep time: 15 minutes
Chill time: 2 hours

■ Lemon Meringue Pie

1 package (3 ounces) JELL-O Pie
    Filling, Lemon Flavor
1 cup sugar
2¼ cups water
3 egg yolks
2 tablespoons lemon juice
2 tablespoons PARKAY Margarine
1 baked 9-inch pie shell, cooled
3 egg whites

COMBINE pie filling mix, ⅔ cup of the sugar and ¼ cup of the water in medium saucepan. Stir in egg yolks and remaining 2 cups water. Cook and stir over medium heat until mixture comes to full boil. Remove from heat. Stir in lemon juice and margarine. Cool 5 minutes, stirring twice. Pour into pie shell.

BEAT egg whites until foamy. Gradually beat in the remaining ⅓ cup sugar; continue beating until stiff peaks form. Spread over pie filling, sealing edges well. Bake at 425° for 5 to 10 minutes or until meringue is lightly browned. Cool at room temperature at least 4 hours before cutting to serve.

MAKES 8 servings

Prep time: 20 minutes
Baking time: 5 minutes

■ Easy German Sweet Chocolate Cake

1 package (2-layer size) yellow cake mix
1 package (4-serving size) JELL-O Instant Pudding and Pie Filling, Vanilla Flavor
1 package (4 ounces) BAKER'S GERMAN'S Sweet Chocolate, melted
4 eggs
1¼ cups buttermilk or milk
¼ cup vegetable oil
Coconut-Pecan Frosting (recipe follows)

COMBINE cake mix, pudding mix, chocolate, eggs, buttermilk and oil in large bowl. Beat at low speed of electric mixer just to moisten, scraping sides of bowl often. Beat at medium speed 4 minutes. Pour into 3 greased and floured 8- or 9-inch layer pans.

BAKE at 350° for 30 minutes or until cake tester inserted in centers comes out clean and cake begins to pull away from sides of pan. (Do not underbake.) Cool in pans 15 minutes. Remove from pans; finish cooling on racks. Spread Coconut-Pecan Frosting between layers and over top of cake.

MAKES 12 servings

Coconut-Pecan Frosting

1 cup evaporated milk or heavy cream
1 cup sugar
3 egg yolks, slightly beaten
½ cup (1 stick) PARKAY Margarine
1 teaspoon vanilla
1⅓ cups (3½ ounces) BAKER'S ANGEL FLAKE Coconut
1 cup chopped pecans

COMBINE evaporated milk, sugar, egg yolks, margarine and vanilla in medium saucepan. Cook and stir over medium heat until mixture thickens, about 12 minutes. Remove from heat. Stir in coconut and pecans. Cool until frosting is of spreading consistency.

MAKES about 2½ cups

Prep time: 30 minutes
Baking time: 30 minutes

■ Coconut Cream Pie

1⅓ cups (3½ ounces) BAKER'S ANGEL FLAKE Coconut
1 baked 9-inch pie shell, cooled
2⅔ cups cold milk
1 package (6-serving size) JELL-O Instant Pudding and Pie Filling, French Vanilla or Vanilla Flavor
1¾ cups (4 ounces) COOL WHIP Whipped Topping, thawed

SPRINKLE ⅔ cup of the coconut onto bottom of pie shell; set aside.

POUR milk into small bowl. Add pie filling mix. Beat with wire whisk until well blended, 1 to 2 minutes. (Mixture will be thin.) Immediately pour over coconut in pie shell. Chill about 1 hour. Spread whipped topping over pie; sprinkle with remaining coconut.

MAKES 8 servings

Prep time: 10 minutes
Chill time: 1 hour

■ Chocolate Mint Dream Pie

**2 envelopes DREAM WHIP Whipped
Topping Mix**
2½ cups cold milk
**2 packages (4-serving size) JELL-O
Instant Pudding and Pie Filling,
Chocolate Flavor**
**3 tablespoons white creme de
menthe liqueur***
**1 packaged chocolate crumb crust
Mint leaves (optional)**

COMBINE whipped topping mix with
1 cup of the milk in large bowl. Beat at
high speed of electric mixer until
topping thickens and forms stiff peaks,
about 6 minutes. Add remaining

1½ cups milk, the pudding mix and
liqueur; blend at low speed. Beat at
high speed for 2 minutes, scraping
sides of bowl occasionally.

SPOON filling mixture into crust. Chill at
least 4 hours or overnight. Garnish with
additional whipped topping and mint
leaves, if desired.

MAKES 8 servings

*¼ teaspoon peppermint extract may
be substituted for creme de menthe
liqueur.

Prep time: 10 minutes
Chill time: 4 hours

Double Pistachio Cake Deluxe

1 package (2-layer size) white or
    yellow cake mix
1 package (4-serving size) JELL-O
    Instant Pudding and Pie Filling,
    Pistachio Flavor
4 eggs
1 cup water
¼ cup vegetable oil
¼ cup chopped nuts
    Fluffy Pistachio Frosting (recipe
    follows)

COMBINE cake mix, pudding mix,
eggs, water and oil in large bowl. Beat
at low speed of electric mixer just to
moisten, scraping sides of bowl often.
Beat at medium speed 4 minutes. Stir
in nuts. Pour into greased and floured
10-inch tube or fluted tube pan. Bake
at 350° for 55 minutes or until cake
tester inserted in center comes out
clean and cake begins to pull away
from sides of pan. (Do not underbake.)
Cool in pan 15 minutes. Remove from
pan; finish cooling on rack. Split cake
into 3 layers. Fill and frost cake with
Fluffy Pistachio Frosting.

MAKES 12 servings

Fluffy Pistachio Frosting

1 cup cold milk
1 package (4-serving size) JELL-O
    Instant Pudding and Pie Filling,
    Pistachio Flavor
¼ cup confectioners sugar
    (optional)
3½ cups (8 ounces) COOL WHIP
    Whipped Topping, thawed

POUR milk into large bowl. Add
pudding mix and the confectioners
sugar. Beat with wire whisk until well
blended, 1 to 2 minutes. Fold in
whipped topping. Spread on cake
immediately. *MAKES about 4 cups*

Note: Store frosted cake in refrigerator.

Prep time: 25 minutes
Baking time: 55 minutes

Dream Cake

1 package (2-layer size) yellow
    cake mix*
1 package (4-serving size) JELL-O
    Pudding and Pie Filling, Vanilla
    Flavor*
1 envelope DREAM WHIP Whipped
    Topping Mix
3 eggs
1 cup water*
¼ cup vegetable oil

COMBINE cake mix, pudding mix,
whipped topping mix, eggs, water
and oil in large bowl. Beat at low
speed of electric mixer just to moisten,
scraping sides of bowl often. Beat at
medium speed 4 minutes. Pour into 2
greased and floured 9-inch layer pans
(each at least 1½ inches deep).

BAKE at 350° for 35 minutes or until
cake tester inserted near centers
comes out clean. Cool in pans 10
minutes. Remove from pans; finish
cooling on racks. Frost as desired.

MAKES 12 servings

*Devil's food cake mix and chocolate
flavor pudding and pie filling may be
substituted for yellow cake mix and
vanilla flavor pudding. Increase water
to 1¼ cups.

Prep time: 20 minutes
Baking time: 35 minutes

Strawberry Sour Cream Pie

1 package (4-serving size) JELL-O Instant Pudding and Pie Filling, French Vanilla or Vanilla Flavor
1 cup (½ pint) sour cream
½ cup cold milk
2 teaspoons grated orange or lemon rind
2 cups thawed COOL WHIP Whipped Topping
1 baked 9-inch pie shell or graham cracker crumb crust, cooled
1 pint strawberries, stems removed

COMBINE pie filling mix, sour cream, milk, rind and whipped topping in medium bowl. Beat with wire whisk until well blended, 1 to 2 minutes. Spoon ½ of the filling into pie shell. Arrange strawberries, stem-ends down, in filling; press down gently. Top with remaining filling.

CHILL pie until set, about 3 hours. Garnish with additional whipped topping and strawberries, if desired.
MAKES 8 servings

Prep time: 15 minutes
Chill time: 3 hours

Better Than S _ X Cake!

1½ cups graham cracker crumbs
6 tablespoons sugar
½ cup (1 stick) PARKAY Margarine, melted
⅔ cup chopped pecans
1 package (8 ounces) PHILADELPHIA BRAND Cream Cheese, softened
3 cups cold milk
1 package (6-serving size) JELL-O Instant Pudding and Pie Filling, French Vanilla or Vanilla Flavor
1⅓ cups (3½ ounces) BAKER'S ANGEL FLAKE Coconut
3½ cups (8 ounces) COOL WHIP Whipped Topping, thawed

COMBINE crumbs, sugar and margarine in medium bowl; mix well. Add ⅓ cup of the pecans. Press mixture evenly onto bottom of 13x9-inch pan.

BEAT cream cheese at low speed of electric mixer until smooth. Gradually beat in ½ cup of the milk. Add pudding mix and remaining 2½ cups milk. Beat at low speed until well blended, 1 to 2 minutes. Stir in 1 cup of the coconut. Immediately pour over crust. Spread whipped topping evenly over pudding mixture. Chill 2 hours.

TOAST remaining ⅓ cup coconut (see page 21 for directions). Sprinkle toasted coconut and remaining pecans over top of dessert.
MAKES 12 servings

Note: Pecans for garnish may be toasted, if desired (see page 19 for directions).

Prep time: 40 minutes
Chill time: 2 hours

■ German Sweet Chocolate Pie

1 frozen 9-inch deep-dish pie shell, thawed and pierced with fork
⅓ cup PARKAY Margarine
⅓ cup firmly packed brown sugar
⅓ cup chopped pecans
⅓ cup BAKER'S ANGEL FLAKE Coconut
1 package (6-serving size) JELL-O Pudding and Pie Filling, Chocolate, French Vanilla or Vanilla Flavor
1 package (4 ounces) BAKER'S GERMAN'S Sweet Chocolate, broken into pieces
2½ cups milk
1 cup thawed COOL WHIP Whipped Topping

BAKE pie shell at 425° for 5 to 8 minutes or until shell begins to brown. Remove from oven.

COMBINE margarine, brown sugar, pecans and coconut in small saucepan. Heat until margarine and sugar are melted, stirring occasionally. Spread mixture onto bottom of hot pie shell. Return to oven for 5 minutes or until bubbly. Cool on rack.

COMBINE pie filling mix, chocolate and milk in medium saucepan. Cook and stir over medium heat until mixture comes to full boil. Cool 5 minutes, stirring twice. Pour over coconut mixture in shell. Cover surface with plastic wrap. Chill about 4 hours. Remove plastic wrap. Garnish with whipped topping. Sprinkle with additional coconut, if desired.

MAKES 8 servings

Prep time: 30 minutes
Baking time: 10 minutes
Chill time: 4 hours

■ Southern Banana Pudding

1 package (4-serving size) JELL-O Pudding and Pie Filling, Banana Cream, French Vanilla or Vanilla Flavor
2 egg yolks, slightly beaten
2½ cups milk
25 vanilla wafers
2 large bananas, sliced
2 egg whites
¼ cup sugar

COMBINE pudding mix, egg yolks and milk in medium saucepan. Cook and stir over medium heat until mixture comes to full boil. Remove from heat. Arrange layer of vanilla wafers on bottom of 1½-quart baking dish. Add layer of banana slices and pudding mixture. Continue layering wafers, bananas and pudding, ending with pudding.

BEAT egg whites until foamy. Gradually beat in sugar; continue beating until stiff peaks form. Spoon over pudding, sealing edges well. Bake at 425° for 5 to 10 minutes or until meringue is lightly browned. Serve warm or chill until ready to serve.

MAKES 8 servings

Prep time: 30 minutes
Baking time: 5 minutes

Rum-Nut Pudding Cake

1 cup chopped pecans or walnuts
1 package (2-layer size) yellow
    cake mix
1 package (4-serving size) JELL-O
    Instant Pudding and Pie Filling,
    Vanilla or Butter Pecan Flavor
4 eggs
¾ cup water
⅔ cup rum
¼ cup vegetable oil
1 cup sugar
½ cup (1 stick) PARKAY Margarine

SPRINKLE nuts evenly onto bottom of greased and floured 10-inch tube or fluted tube pan.

COMBINE cake mix, pudding mix, eggs, ½ cup of the water, ⅓ cup of the rum and oil in large bowl. Beat at low speed of electric mixer just to moisten, scraping sides of bowl often. Beat at medium speed 4 minutes. Pour over nuts in pan. Bake at 325° for 1 hour or until cake tester inserted in center comes out clean and cake begins to pull away from sides of pan. (Do not underbake.) Cool in pan 15 minutes.

COMBINE sugar, margarine and remaining ¼ cup water in small saucepan. Cook and stir over medium-high heat until mixture comes to boil. Boil 5 minutes, stirring constantly. Stir in remaining ⅓ cup rum; return just to boil. Invert cake onto serving plate; pierce in several places with cake tester or wooden pick. Carefully spoon warm syrup over warm cake.   *MAKES 12 servings*

Prep time: 30 minutes
Baking time: 1 hour

Easy Grasshopper Pie

1 package (4-serving size) JELL-O
    Brand Gelatin, Lime Flavor
1 cup boiling water
¼ cup cold water
2 tablespoons green creme de
    menthe liqueur
2 tablespoons white creme de
    cacao liqueur
1¾ cups (4 ounces) COOL WHIP
    Whipped Topping, thawed
1 prepared chocolate or graham
    cracker crumb crust

DISSOLVE gelatin in boiling water. Add cold water and liqueurs. Chill until slightly thickened. Fold in whipped topping.

SPOON gelatin mixture into crust. Chill until firm, about 3 hours. Garnish with additional whipped topping or Chocolate Curls (see page 22 for directions), if desired.
MAKES 8 servings

Prep time: 20 minutes
Chill time: 3 hours

"Look Jane, Jerry brought it!"

JELL-O®

America's most famous dessert

Circa 1925

FAMILY FAVORITES

■ Waldorf Salad

2 packages (4-serving size each) or
    1 package (8-serving size)
    JELL-O Brand Gelatin, Lemon
    Flavor
1½ cups boiling water
  1 tablespoon lemon juice
  1 cup cold water
    Ice cubes
  ½ cup MIRACLE WHIP Salad Dressing
1½ cups diced apples
  ¾ cup diced celery
  ¼ cup chopped walnuts

DISSOLVE gelatin in boiling water. Add lemon juice. Combine cold water and ice cubes to make 2 cups. Add to gelatin, stirring until slightly thickened. Remove any unmelted ice. Stir in salad dressing with wire whisk; chill until thickened.

FOLD apples, celery and walnuts into gelatin mixture. Pour into 5-cup mold. Chill until firm, about 3 hours. Unmold. Serve with crisp salad greens and additional salad dressing, if desired.

MAKES 10 servings

Prep time: 20 minutes
Chill time: 3 hours

■ Muffin Pan Snacks

1 package (4-serving size) JELL-O
    Brand Gelatin, any flavor
¾ cup boiling water
½ cup cold water
    Ice cubes
1½ cups diced fresh fruit or
    vegetables

DISSOLVE gelatin in boiling water. Combine cold water and ice cubes to make 1 cup. Add to gelatin, stirring until slightly thickened. Remove any unmelted ice. Add fruit. Chill until thickened, about 10 minutes.

PLACE foil baking cups in muffin pans, or use small individual molds. Spoon gelatin mixture into cups or molds, filling each about ⅔ full. Chill until firm, about 2 hours.

PEEL away foil cups carefully or dip molds in warm water for about 5 seconds to unmold.

MAKES 6 servings

Prep time: 15 minutes
Chill time: 2 hours

Muffin Pan Snacks

■ Pineapple-Cream Cheese Mold

1 can (8 ounces) crushed
    pineapple in juice, undrained
1 package (4-serving size) JELL-O
    Brand Gelatin, Lemon or Lime
    Flavor
1 cup boiling water
1 tablespoon lemon juice
1 package (3 ounces)
    PHILADELPHIA BRAND Cream
    Cheese, softened
¼ cup chopped walnuts

DRAIN pineapple, reserving juice. Add cold water to juice to make ¾ cup. Dissolve gelatin in boiling water. Add measured liquid and lemon juice. Gradually add 1 cup of the gelatin to cream cheese, blending well. Chill until thickened. Stir in walnuts. Pour into 4-cup mold or individual molds. Chill until set, but not firm. Chill remaining gelatin until thickened. Fold in pineapple. Spoon over set gelatin in mold.

CHILL until firm, about 3 hours. Unmold. Serve as dessert with whipped topping, or as salad, if desired.

MAKES 6 servings

Prep time: 20 minutes
Chill time: 3 hours

■ Florida Sunshine Salad

½ cup fresh orange sections, halved
½ cup fresh grapefruit sections,
    halved
1 tablespoon sugar
1 package (4-serving size) JELL-O
    Brand Gelatin, Orange or
    Lemon Flavor
1 cup boiling water
    Citrus Twist (see page 17 for
    directions) (optional)
    Mint leaves (optional)

SPRINKLE fruit with sugar; let stand 10 to 15 minutes. Drain, reserving liquid. Add cold water to liquid to make ¾ cup.

DISSOLVE gelatin in boiling water. Add measured liquid. Measure ¾ cup gelatin into small bowl; set aside. Chill remaining gelatin until thickened. Fold in drained fruit. Pour gelatin mixture into serving bowl. Chill until set but not firm.

PLACE small bowl of measured gelatin in larger bowl of ice and water. Stir until slightly thickened. Beat at high speed of electric mixer until fluffy, thick and about doubled in volume. Spoon over gelatin in bowl. Chill until firm, about 4 hours. Garnish with Citrus Twist and mint leaves, if desired.

MAKES 6 servings

Prep time: 20 minutes
Chill time: 4 hours

Florida Sunshine Salad

Tuna Salad Mold

1 package (4-serving size) JELL-O Brand Gelatin, Lemon or Lime Flavor
½ teaspoon salt
1 cup boiling water
¾ cup cold water
2 teaspoons vinegar
1 can (7 ounces) tuna, drained and flaked
2 hard-cooked eggs, chopped
½ cup chopped dill pickles (optional)
¼ cup diced celery
2 tablespoons chopped scallions

DISSOLVE gelatin and salt in boiling water. Add cold water and vinegar. Chill until slightly thickened. Fold in tuna, eggs, pickles, celery and scallions. Pour into 4-cup mold. Chill until firm, about 4 hours. Unmold. Serve on crisp salad greens, if desired.
MAKES 4 servings

Prep time: 25 minutes
Chill time: 4 hours

Yogurt Garden Salad

1 package (4-serving size) JELL-O Brand Gelatin, Lemon Flavor
1 cup boiling water
1 tablespoon vinegar
1 container (8 ounces) plain yogurt
1 cup grated carrots
½ cup chopped green pepper
1 tablespoon chopped scallions

DISSOLVE gelatin in boiling water. Add vinegar. Chill until slightly thickened.

Blend in yogurt. Fold in carrots, green pepper and scallions. Pour into 3-cup mold or individual molds. Chill until firm, about 3 hours. Unmold.
MAKES 4 to 6 servings

Prep time: 20 minutes
Chill time: 3 hours

Spicy Chicken Spread

1 package (4-serving size) JELL-O Brand Gelatin, Lemon Flavor
1 cup boiling water
1 package (8 ounces) PHILADELPHIA BRAND Cream Cheese, softened
1 cup (½ pint) sour cream
½ cup MIRACLE WHIP Salad Dressing
2 ounces blue cheese, finely crumbled
2 teaspoons hot pepper sauce
1 teaspoon vinegar
2 cans (5 ounces each) chunk white chicken in water, drained and finely chopped (about 1½ cups)
Assorted crackers and fresh vegetables

DISSOLVE gelatin in boiling water. Beat cream cheese in large bowl at medium speed of electric mixer until smooth. Add sour cream, salad dressing, blue cheese, hot pepper sauce and vinegar; beat until smooth. Gradually stir in gelatin. Chill until thickened. Fold in chicken. Spoon into 5-cup mold. Chill until firm, about 4 hours. Unmold. Serve with crackers and vegetables.   *MAKES 5 cups*

Prep time: 20 minutes
Chill time: 4 hours

■ Cucumber Sour Cream Mold

**2 packages (4-serving size each) or
    1 package (8-serving size)
    JELL-O Brand Gelatin, Lime
    Flavor**
¼ teaspoon salt
1½ cups boiling water
1½ cups cold water
2 tablespoons lemon juice
½ cup MIRACLE WHIP Salad Dressing
½ cup sour cream
**1½ cups chopped, seeded, peeled
    cucumbers**
2 tablespoons minced onion
1 teaspoon dillweed*

DISSOLVE gelatin and salt in boiling water. Add cold water and lemon juice; chill until slightly thickened.

COMBINE salad dressing and sour cream in large bowl until well blended. Gradually stir in gelatin with wire whisk. Chill until thickened. Fold in cucumbers, onion and dillweed. Pour into 5-cup mold. Chill until firm, about 4 hours. Unmold. Serve with crisp salad greens, if desired.

MAKES 10 servings

*1 tablespoon minced fresh dill may be substituted for dillweed.

Prep time: 20 minutes
Chill time: 4 hours

■ Cranberry Sour Cream Delight

**2 packages (4-serving size each) or
    1 package (8-serving size)
    JELL-O Brand Gelatin, any red
    flavor**
2 cups boiling water
**1 can (16 ounces) jellied or whole
    berry cranberry sauce**
**1 tablespoon grated orange rind
    (optional)**
1 cup (½ pint) sour cream

DISSOLVE gelatin in boiling water. Add cranberry sauce to gelatin in small amounts; stir until cranberry sauce is melted. Stir in orange rind and sour cream. Pour into 5-cup mold or individual molds. Chill until firm, about 4 hours. Unmold.

MAKES 10 servings

Prep time: 15 minutes
Chill time: 4 hours

▪ Creamy Fruit Salad

1 can (11 ounces) mandarin
    orange sections, undrained
1 package (4-serving size) JELL-O
    Brand Gelatin, any flavor
1 cup boiling water
1 cup (½ pint) sour cream
½ cup MIRACLE WHIP Salad Dressing
1 can (8 ounces) crushed
    pineapple, drained
1 cup KRAFT Miniature
    Marshmallows
½ cup chopped nuts

DRAIN orange sections, reserving syrup. Add water to syrup to make ½ cup. Dissolve gelatin in boiling water. Add measured liquid. Chill until slightly thickened. Stir in sour cream and salad dressing until well blended. Chill until thickened.

STIR orange sections, pineapple, marshmallows and nuts into gelatin mixture. Pour into 5-cup mold. Chill until firm, about 4 hours. Unmold.

MAKES 10 servings

Prep time: 20 minutes
Chill time: 4 hours

▪ Cookies and Cream Pie

Chocolate sandwich cookies
1½ cups cold milk
1 cup ice cream, any flavor,
    softened
1 package (6-serving size) JELL-O
    Instant Pudding and Pie Filling,
    any flavor
COOL WHIP Whipped Topping,
    thawed (optional)

LINE bottom and sides of 9-inch pie plate with cookies.

BLEND milk and ice cream in medium bowl. Add pie filling mix. Beat with wire whisk or at low speed of electric mixer until blended, 1 to 2 minutes. Pour immediately into pie plate. Chill until set, about 3 hours. Garnish with whipped topping, if desired.

MAKES 8 servings

Prep time: 15 minutes
Chill time: 3 hours

Cookies and Cream Pie

■ Berried Delight

1½ cups graham cracker crumbs
½ cup sugar
⅓ cup PARKAY Margarine, melted
1 package (8 ounces)
    PHILADELPHIA BRAND Cream
    Cheese, softened
2⅔ cups cold milk
3½ cups (8 ounces) COOL WHIP
    Whipped Topping, thawed
2 pints strawberries, hulled and
    halved
1 package (6-serving size) JELL-O
    Instant Pudding and Pie Filling,
    French Vanilla or Vanilla Flavor

COMBINE crumbs and ¼ cup of the sugar. Mix in margarine. Press mixture evenly onto bottom of 13×9-inch pan. (If desired, bake at 375° for 8 minutes. Cool on rack.)

BEAT cream cheese with remaining ¼ cup sugar and 2 tablespoons of the milk until smooth. Fold in ½ of the whipped topping. Spread over crust. Arrange strawberries in even layer on cream cheese mixture.

POUR the remaining milk into medium bowl. Add pudding mix. Beat with wire whisk until well blended, 1 to 2 minutes. Pour over strawberries. Chill 4 hours or overnight.

SPREAD remaining whipped topping over pudding just before serving. Garnish with additional strawberries, if desired.   *MAKES 18 servings*

Prep time: 35 minutes
Baking time: 8 minutes
Chill time: 4 hours

Top: Striped Delight; bottom: Berried Delight

■ Striped Delight

1 cup all-purpose flour
1 cup finely chopped pecans
¾ cup sugar
½ cup PARKAY Margarine, melted
1 package (8 ounces)
    PHILADELPHIA BRAND Cream
    Cheese, softened
2⅔ cups cold milk
3½ cups (8 ounces) COOL WHIP
    Whipped Topping, thawed
1 package (6-serving size) JELL-O
    Instant Pudding and Pie Filling,
    any flavor
    Chocolate Curls (see page 22 for
    directions) (optional)

COMBINE flour, pecans, ½ cup of the sugar and margarine; mix until flour is moistened. Press mixture evenly onto bottom of 13×9-inch pan. Bake at 350° for 20 minutes or until lightly browned. Cool on rack.

BEAT cream cheese with remaining ¼ cup sugar and 2 tablespoons of the milk until smooth. Fold in ½ of the whipped topping. Spread over cooled crust.

POUR the remaining milk into medium bowl. Add pudding mix. Beat with wire whisk until well blended, 1 to 2 minutes. Pour over cream cheese layer. Chill 4 hours or overnight.

SPREAD remaining whipped topping over pudding just before serving. Garnish with Chocolate Curls, if desired.   *MAKES 18 servings*

Prep time: 30 minutes
Baking time: 20 minutes
Chill time: 4 hours

■ Pudding Poke Cake

1 package (2-layer size) yellow or
    chocolate cake mix
2 packages (4-serving size each)
    JELL-O Instant Pudding and Pie
    Filling, any flavor
1 cup confectioners sugar
4 cups cold milk

PREPARE cake mix as directed on
package, baking in 13x9-inch pan.
Remove from oven. Immediately poke
holes down through cake to pan with
round handle of wooden spoon. (Or
poke holes with a plastic drinking
straw, using a turning motion to make
large holes.) Holes should be at 1-inch
intervals.

COMBINE pudding mix with sugar in
large bowl after holes are made.
Gradually stir in milk. Beat at low
speed of electric mixer for not more
than 1 minute. (Do not overbeat.)
Quickly, before pudding mixture
thickens, pour about ½ of the thin
pudding mixture evenly over warm
cake and into holes to make stripes.
Allow remaining pudding mixture to
thicken slightly; spoon over top,
swirling to "frost" the cake. Chill at
least 1 hour. Store cake in refrigerator.

MAKES 18 servings

Prep time: 30 minutes
Chill time: 1 hour

■ Double Chocolate Bread Pudding

1 package (4-serving size) JELL-O Pudding and Pie Filling, Chocolate Flavor
2½ cups milk
3 cups French bread cubes
1 cup BAKER'S Semi-Sweet Real Chocolate Chips
1 teaspoon vanilla

COMBINE pudding mix and milk, stirring until well blended. Stir in bread cubes, chocolate chips and vanilla. Pour into 12×8-inch microwavable baking dish. Microwave on HIGH 9 minutes or until mixture comes to boil, stirring twice during cooking time. Remove from microwave oven. Let stand 10 minutes before serving.

MAKES 8 servings

Note: Ovens vary; cooking time is approximate.

Conventional Oven Preparation:
Assemble recipe as directed. Bake at 375° for 40 minutes or until mixture comes to boil. Remove from oven. Let stand 10 minutes before serving.

Prep time: 15 minutes
Baking time: 9 minutes, microwave; 40 minutes, conventional over

■ Apple Raisin Bread Pudding

8 to 10 slices cinnamon-raisin bread
2 medium apples, peeled and chopped
¼ cup sugar
¼ teaspoon ground cinnamon
⅛ teaspoon ground nutmeg
1 package (4-serving size) JELL-O Pudding and Pie Filling, Vanilla Flavor
2 cups milk

SLICE bread in half diagonally. Combine apples, sugar and spices; sprinkle ½ of the mixture into 12×8-inch microwavable baking dish. Arrange bread over apples in baking dish, overlapping slices. Sprinkle with remaining apple mixture.

COMBINE pudding mix and milk, stirring until well blended. Pour over apples and bread. Microwave on HIGH 5 minutes. Rotate dish half turn; press bread into pudding with back of spoon. Microwave 2 to 3 minutes longer or until mixture comes to boil. Remove from microwave oven. Let stand 10 minutes before serving.

MAKES 8 servings

Note: Ovens vary; cooking time is approximate.

Conventional Oven Preparation:
Assemble recipe as directed. Bake at 375° for 25 minutes or until mixture comes to boil. Remove from oven. Let stand 10 minutes before serving.

Prep time: 15 minutes
Baking time: 8 minutes, microwave; 25 minutes, conventional oven

■ Pudding Chip Cookies

1 cup PARKAY Margarine, softened
¾ cup firmly packed light brown
    sugar
¼ cup granulated sugar
1 package (4-serving size) JELL-O
    Instant Pudding and Pie Filling,
    Butter Pecan, Butterscotch,
    Chocolate, Milk Chocolate,
    Chocolate Fudge, French
    Vanilla or Vanilla Flavor
1 teaspoon vanilla
2 eggs
2¼ cups all-purpose flour
1 teaspoon baking soda
1 package (12 ounces) BAKER'S
    Semi-Sweet Real Chocolate
    Chips
1 cup chopped nuts (optional)

BEAT margarine, sugars, pudding mix and vanilla in large bowl until smooth and creamy. Beat in eggs. Gradually add flour and baking soda. Stir in chips and nuts. (Dough will be stiff.) Drop by teaspoonfuls 2 inches apart onto ungreased baking sheets. Bake at 375° for 8 to 10 minutes or until lightly browned. Remove; cool on racks.
    MAKES about 7 dozen cookies

Prep time: 30 minutes
Baking time: 30 minutes

■ Fruit Flavor Freeze

1 package (4-serving size) Jell-O
    Brand Gelatin, any flavor
¾ cup sugar
1 cup boiling water
2 cups milk
1¾ cups (4 ounces) COOL WHIP
    Whipped Topping, thawed
    Assorted cookies (optional)

DISSOLVE gelatin and sugar in boiling water. Stir in milk. (Mixture will appear curdled but will be smooth when frozen.) Pour into 13×9-inch pan. Freeze until ice crystals form 1 inch around edge, about 1 hour.

SPOON gelatin mixture into chilled bowl. Beat until smooth. Blend in whipped topping. Return to pan. Freeze until firm, about 4 hours. Serve with assorted cookies, if desired.
    MAKES 10 servings

Prep time: 15 minutes
Freezing time: 5 hours

Fruit Flavor Freeze

■ Chocolate Turtle Pie

¼ cup caramel or butterscotch
    flavor dessert topping
1 baked 8- or 9-inch pie shell,
    cooled
¾ cup pecan halves
1 package (4-serving size) JELL-O
    Pudding and Pie Filling,
    Chocolate Flavor*
1¾ cups milk*
1¾ cups (4 ounces) COOL WHIP
    Whipped Topping, thawed

BRING caramel topping to boil in small
saucepan, stirring constantly. Pour into
pie shell. Arrange pecans on top; chill.

COMBINE pie filling mix and milk in
medium saucepan. Cook and stir over
medium heat until mixture comes to
full boil. Cool 5 minutes, stirring twice.
Pour into pie shell; place plastic wrap
on surface of filling. Chill 3 hours.
Remove plastic wrap. Cover with
whipped topping. Drizzle with
additional caramel topping and
garnish with additional pecans, if
desired.   *MAKES 8 servings*

*1 package (4-serving size) instant
pudding may be substituted for
1 package (4-serving size) cooked
pudding mix. Prepare as directed on
package, using 1½ cups *cold* milk.

Prep time: 15 minutes
Chill time: 3 hours

■ Vanilla Rice Pudding

4 cups milk
1 egg, well beaten
1 package (4-serving size) JELL-O
    Pudding and Pie Filling, French
    Vanilla, Vanilla or Coconut
    Cream Flavor
1 cup MINUTE Rice, uncooked
¼ cup raisins (optional)
¼ teaspoon ground cinnamon
⅛ teaspoon ground nutmeg

STIR milk and egg gradually into
pudding mix in medium saucepan.
Add rice and raisins. Cook and stir
over medium heat until mixture just
comes to boil. Cool 5 minutes, stirring
twice. Pour into dessert dishes or
serving bowl. Sprinkle with cinnamon
and nutmeg. Serve warm.
              MAKES 10 servings

Note: For chilled pudding, place
plastic wrap on surface of hot
pudding; cool slightly. Chill about 1
hour. Stir before serving. Sprinkle with
cinnamon and nutmeg.

Prep time: 20 minutes

Circa 1905

UNDER 100 CALORIES

Melon Bubbles

1 package (4-serving size) JELL-O
   Brand Sugar Free Gelatin, any
   flavor
¾ cup boiling water
½ cup cold water
   Ice cubes
1 cup melon balls (cantaloupe,
   honeydew or watermelon)
   Mint leaves (optional)

DISSOLVE gelatin in boiling water.
Combine cold water and ice cubes to
make 1¼ cups. Add to gelatin, stirring
until slightly thickened. Remove any
unmelted ice. Measure 1⅓ cups
gelatin into small bowl; add melon.
Pour into individual dessert glasses or
serving bowl.

WHIP remaining gelatin at high speed
of electric mixer until fluffy, thick and
about doubled in volume. Spoon over
gelatin in glasses. Chill until set, about
2 hours. Garnish with additional melon
balls and mint leaves, if desired.
   MAKES 7 (½-cup) servings,
   about 12 calories per serving

Prep time: 10 minutes
Chill time: 2 hours

Melon Bubbles

JELL-O Sugar Free Jigglers
Gelatin Snacks

2½ cups boiling water
  4 packages (4-serving size each) or 2 packages (8-serving size each) JELL-O Brand Sugar Free Gelatin, any flavor

ADD boiling water to gelatin. Dissolve completely. Pour into 13×9-inch pan. Chill until firm, about 3 hours.

DIP pan in warm water about 15 seconds for easy removal. Cut gelatin into 1-inch cubes. (Or use cookie cutters to cut decorative shapes; cut remaining gelatin into cubes.)

MAKES about 8 dozen cubes,
about 2 calories per cube

Prep time: 10 minutes
Chill time: 3 hours

Notes: For thicker JELL-O Sugar Free Jigglers, use 8- or 9-inch square pan.

To use ice cube trays or JELL-O Jiggler molds, pour gelatin mixture into 2 or 3 ice cube trays. Chill until firm, about 2 hours. To remove, dip trays in warm water about 15 seconds. Moisten tips of fingers and gently pull from edges.

JELL-O Fruited Jigglers: Prepare JELL-O Sugar Free Jigglers recipe as directed. Pour dissolved gelatin into 9-inch square pan. Arrange banana slices, strawberry slices or canned pineapple chunks in gelatin so that when cut into cubes, each will contain 1 piece of fruit. Chill until firm, about 3 hours. Cut into cubes. Makes about 3 dozen cubes, **about 8 calories per cube.**

JELL-O Pineapple Jigglers: Prepare JELL-O Sugar Free Jigglers recipe as directed, adding 1 can (8 ounces) crushed pineapple and juice to dissolved gelatin. Pour into 13×9-inch pan. Chill until firm, about 3 hours. Cut into cubes. Makes about 8 dozen cubes, **about 2 calories per cube.**

JELL-O Yogurt Jigglers: Prepare Sugar Free Jigglers recipe as directed. Cool gelatin to room temperature. Stir 2 containers (8 ounces each) of plain lowfat yogurt into gelatin with wire whisk until well blended. Pour into 13×9-inch pan. Chill until firm, about 3 hours. Cut into cubes. Makes about 8 dozen cubes, **about 4 calories per cube.**

JELL-O Sugar Free Jigglers and JELL-O Yogurt Jigglers

JELL-O Creamy Sugar Free Jigglers
Gelatin Snacks

2½ cups boiling water
  4 packages (4-serving size each) or
    2 packages (8-serving size
    each) JELL-O Brand Sugar Free
    Gelatin, any flavor
2½ cups boiling water
  1 cup cold lowfat milk
  1 package (4-serving size) JELL-O
    Sugar Free Instant Pudding and
    Pie Filling, Vanilla Flavor

ADD boiling water to gelatin. Dissolve completely; cool to room temperature.

POUR milk into small bowl. Add pudding mix. Beat with wire whisk until well blended, 1 to 2 minutes. Quickly pour into gelatin. Stir with wire whisk until well blended. Pour into 13×9-inch pan. Chill until firm, about 3 hours.

DIP pan in warm water about 15 seconds for easy removal. Cut gelatin into 1-inch cubes. (Or use cookie cutters to cut decorative shapes; cut remaining gelatin into cubes.)
MAKES about 8 dozen cubes, about 4 calories per cube

Prep time: 15 minutes
Chill time: 3 hours

JELL-O Vegetable Jigglers
Gelatin Snacks

2½ cups boiling water
  4 packages (4-serving size each) or
    2 packages (8-serving size
    each) JELL-O Brand Sugar Free
    Gelatin, Lemon, Lime or Orange
    Flavor
  ½ cup shredded carrot
  ½ cup finely chopped celery
  ½ cup finely chopped cucumber
  3 tablespoons vinegar

ADD boiling water to gelatin. Dissolve completely. Stir in vegetables and vinegar. Pour into 13×9-inch pan. Chill until firm, about 3 hours.

DIP pan in warm water about 15 seconds for easy removal. Cut gelatin into 1-inch cubes. (Or use cookie cutters to cut decorative shapes; cut remaining gelatin into cubes.)
MAKES about 8 dozen cubes, about 2 calories per cube

Prep time: 15 minutes
Chill time: 3 hours

Lemon Cheesecake Cups

1 package (4-serving size) JELL-O Brand Sugar Free Gelatin, Lemon Flavor
¾ cup boiling water
3 ounces PHILADELPHIA BRAND LIGHT Neufchatel Cheese, softened and cut into cubes
½ cup cold water
1 teaspoon grated lemon rind (optional)
½ cup thawed COOL WHIP Whipped Topping
  Graham cracker crumbs (optional)
  Lemon slices (optional)
  Mint leaves (optional)

DISSOLVE gelatin in boiling water in blender container; cover. Blend at medium speed 1 minute. Add cream cheese. Blend until smooth, about 1 minute. Add cold water and lemon rind. Cool slightly.

BLEND whipped topping into gelatin mixture. Spoon into dessert dishes. Chill 1 hour. Sprinkle with graham cracker crumbs and garnish with lemon slices and mint leaves, if desired. *MAKES 6 servings, about 60 calories per serving (without garnish)*

Prep time: 15 minutes
Chill time: 1 hour

Chocolate Mousse

1½ cups cold lowfat milk
1 package (4-serving size) JELL-O Sugar Free Instant Pudding and Pie Filling, Chocolate Flavor
1 cup thawed COOL WHIP Whipped Topping
Raspberries (optional)
Mint leaves (optional)

POUR milk into small bowl. Add pudding mix. Beat with wire whisk until well blended, 1 to 2 minutes. Fold in whipped topping. Spoon into serving bowl or individual dessert dishes. Chill until ready to serve. Garnish with additional whipped topping, raspberries and mint leaves, if desired.

MAKES 5 (½-cup) servings,
about 100 calories per serving
(without garnish)

Prep time: 5 minutes

Creamy Frozen Yogurt

1 package (4-serving size) JELL-O Brand Sugar Free Gelatin, any flavor
1 cup boiling water
½ cup cold water
1 container (8 ounces) plain lowfat yogurt
2 cups thawed COOL WHIP Whipped Topping

DISSOLVE gelatin in boiling water. Add cold water. Stir in yogurt until well blended and smooth. Fold in whipped topping. Pour into 9-inch square pan. Freeze until firm, about 6 hours or overnight. Scoop into individual dessert dishes.

MAKES 7 (½-cup) servings,
about 80 calories per serving

Prep time: 10 minutes
Freezing time: 6 hours

Chocolate Mousse

Fluffy Yogurt Snack

1 package (4-serving size) JELL-O Brand Sugar Free Gelatin, any flavor
¾ cup boiling water
½ cup cold water
   Ice cubes
1 container (8 ounces) plain lowfat yogurt
½ teaspoon vanilla

DISSOLVE gelatin in boiling water. Combine cold water and ice cubes to make 1 cup. Add to gelatin, stirring until thickened. Remove any unmelted ice. Blend in yogurt and vanilla. Pour into dessert dishes. Chill until set, about 30 minutes.

MAKES 5 (½-cup) servings,
about 40 calories per serving

Prep time: 10 minutes
Chill time: 30 minutes

Fruit Sparkles

1 package (4-serving size) JELL-O Brand Sugar Free Gelatin, any flavor
1 cup boiling water
1 cup cold fruit flavor seltzer, sparkling water, club soda or other sugar free carbonated beverage
1 cup sliced banana and strawberries*
   Mint leaves (optional)

DISSOLVE gelatin in boiling water. Add beverage. Chill until slightly thickened. Add fruit. Pour into individual dessert dishes. Chill until firm, about 1 hour. Garnish with additional fruit and mint leaves, if desired.

MAKES 6 (½-cup) servings,
about 25 calories per serving

*1 cup drained mandarin orange sections or crushed pineapple may be substituted for bananas and strawberries.

Prep time: 15 minutes
Chill time: 1½ hours

Fruit Sparkles

Fresh Fruit Parfait

½ cup blueberries
½ cup sliced strawberries
1 package (4-serving size) JELL-O
    Brand Sugar Free Gelatin, any
    flavor
¾ cup boiling water
½ cup cold water
    Ice cubes
¾ cup thawed COOL WHIP Whipped
    Topping
    Mint leaves (optional)

DIVIDE fruit among 6 parfait glasses. Dissolve gelatin in boiling water. Combine cold water and ice cubes to make 1¼ cups. Add to gelatin, stirring until slightly thickened. Remove any unmelted ice. Measure ¾ cup gelatin; pour over fruit in glasses. Chill until set but not firm.

FOLD whipped topping into remaining gelatin. Spoon into glasses. Chill until set, about 1 hour. Garnish with additional fruit and mint leaves, if desired.

MAKES 6 (½-cup) servings,
about 40 calories per serving

Prep time: 20 minutes
Chill time: 1 hour

Fruit Flavor Popcorn

8 cups popped popcorn
3 tablespoons PARKAY Margarine,
    melted
1 package (4-serving size) JELL-O
    Brand Sugar Free Gelatin, any
    flavor

PLACE popcorn in large bowl. Add melted margarine; toss to coat well. Sprinkle with gelatin; toss until evenly coated.   *MAKES 8 cups,*
about 60 calories per cup

Prep time: 5 minutes

Fresh Fruit Parfait

Fruited Yogurt Shake

3 cups cold lowfat milk
1 package (4-serving size) JELL-O Sugar Free Instant Pudding and Pie Filling, any flavor
1 container (8 ounces) plain lowfat yogurt
1 cup crushed ice
1 medium banana, cut into chunks*

COMBINE all ingredients in blender in order given; cover. Blend at high speed 1 minute. Pour into glasses. Serve immediately.

MAKES about 6 (½-cup) servings,
about 87 calories per serving

*½ cup sliced strawberries may be substituted for banana chunks.

Prep time: 5 minutes

Apple-Cheese Snack

1 package (4-serving size) JELL-O Brand Sugar Free Gelatin, Orange Flavor
¾ cup boiling water
¼ teaspoon ground ginger (optional)
½ cup cold water
Ice cubes
⅓ cup lowfat cottage cheese
1 small apple, cored and diced

DISSOLVE gelatin in boiling water; stir in ginger. Combine cold water and ice cubes to make 1¼ cups. Add to gelatin, stirring until slightly thickened. Remove any unmelted ice. Measure ¾ cup gelatin; pour into blender. Add cottage cheese; cover. Blend until smooth, about 1 minute. Chill about 15 minutes.

STIR apple into remaining gelatin. Spoon into individual dessert glasses. Chill about 10 minutes. Spoon creamy mixture over fruited gelatin. Chill until set, about 30 minutes.

MAKES 6 (½-cup) servings,
about 25 calories per serving

Prep time: 15 minutes
Chill time: 1 hour

The Dainty Dessert

"THE JELL-O GIRL"

Circa 1905

DELICIOUS DRINKS

■ Cranberry-Orange Cooler

1 package (4-serving size) JELL-O
    Brand Gelatin, Orange Flavor
1 cup boiling water
2½ cups cranberry juice, chilled
    Ice cubes (optional)
    Orange slices (optional)

DISSOLVE gelatin in boiling water. Add
cranberry juice. Pour over ice cubes in
tall glasses and garnish with orange
slices, if desired.

*MAKES about 3½ cups
or 4 servings*

Prep time: 5 minutes

---

*Several of the recipes in this
chapter call for alcohol as an
ingredient. We urge you to use
them responsibly. Remember,
drinking and driving don't mix.*

■ Lime Vodka Punch

1 package (4-serving size) JELL-O
    Brand Gelatin, Lime Flavor
1 package (4-serving size) JELL-O
    Brand Gelatin, Lemon Flavor
2 cups boiling water
1 bottle (1 liter) club soda, lemon
    soda or lemon-lime
    carbonated beverage, chilled
1 cup vodka or white wine
    (optional)
1 orange, lemon or lime, thinly
    sliced
    Ice cubes (optional)

DISSOLVE gelatins in boiling water;
cool. (Keep at room temperature until
ready to serve.) Stir in club soda,
vodka and orange slices just before
serving. Serve over ice, if desired.

*MAKES 8 cups
or 16 servings*

Prep time: 10 minutes

*Clockwise from left: Cranberry-Orange
Cooler; Lime Vodka Punch; Strawberry
Ginger Punch (page 214)*

■ Gelatin Shots

Gelatin shots began as a fad several years ago and now have become a popular order in the bar scene. They are usually served in small paper cups and eaten like Italian ices. Try the combinations here, or create some of your own.

**1 package (4-serving size) JELL-O
     Brand Gelatin, any flavor
1 cup boiling water
½ cup cold tequila or vodka
½ cup cold water**

DISSOLVE gelatin in boiling water. Add liquor and cold water. Pour into 12 (2-ounce) souffle cups. Chill until set, about 1 hour. Garnish with assorted fruit, if desired.   *MAKES 12 servings*

Lime-Tequila Shots: Use lime flavor gelatin and tequila.

Strawberry-Vodka Shots: Use strawberry flavor gelatin and vodka.

Prep time: 10 minutes
Chill time: 1 hour

■ "Light" Gelatin Shots

**1 package (4-serving size) JELL-O
     Brand Gelatin, any flavor
1 cup boiling water
½ to ¾ cup cold juice or soda
¼ to ½ cup cold liqueur, rum or wine**

DISSOLVE gelatin in boiling water. Add juice and liqueur. Pour into 12 (2-ounce) souffle cups. Chill until set, about 1 hour.   *MAKES 12 servings*

Cherry-Rum Cola Shots: Use cherry flavor gelatin, ¾ cup cola beverage and ¼ cup rum.

Orange Triplex: Use orange flavor gelatin, ¾ cup orange flavor sparkling water and ¼ cup any orange liqueur.

Raspberry Wine Spritzers: Use raspberry flavor gelatin, ½ cup club soda and ½ cup white wine.

Prep time: 10 minutes
Chill time: 1 hour

Gelatin Shots and "Light" Gelatin Shots

■ Strawberry Ginger Punch

1 package (4-serving size) JELL-O Brand Gelatin, Strawberry Flavor
¼ cup sugar
1½ cups boiling water
2½ cups cold water
1 package (10 ounces) BIRDS EYE Quick Thaw Strawberries
1 can (6 ounces) frozen concentrated lemonade or limeade
1 bottle (1 liter) ginger ale, chilled
Mint leaves
Ice cubes (optional)

DISSOLVE gelatin and sugar in boiling water. Add cold water, strawberries and concentrate; stir until strawberries and concentrate are thawed. Chill until ready to serve. Stir in ginger ale and mint. Serve over ice, if desired.
MAKES 10 cups or 20 servings

Prep time: 10 minutes

■ "Glogg"

1 package (4-serving size) JELL-O Brand Gelatin, any flavor
3 cups boiling water
1 cinnamon stick
6 whole cloves
3 orange slices

DISSOLVE gelatin in boiling water in 4-cup measuring cup. Add cinnamon stick, cloves and orange slices. Cover; let stand 5 minutes. Remove spices and oranges. Pour gelatin mixture into mugs; serve warm. Garnish with additional cinnamon sticks and clove-studded orange slices, if desired.
MAKES about 3 cups or 4 to 6 servings

Prep time: 5 minutes

■ Microwave Hot Chocolate

4 cups milk
1 package (4-serving size) JELL-O Pudding and Pie Filling, Chocolate or Chocolate Fudge Flavor
COOL WHIP Whipped Topping, thawed (optional)
Chocolate Curls (see page 22 for directions) (optional)

POUR milk into 2-quart microwavable bowl. Add pudding mix. Beat with wire whisk until well blended. Microwave on HIGH 5 minutes; whisk again. Pour into mugs. Top with whipped topping and garnish with Chocolate Curls, if desired.
MAKES about 4 cups or 4 servings

Prep time: 5 minutes
Cooking time: 5 minutes

Top: "Glogg;" bottom: Microwave Hot Chocolate

■ Frosty Pudding Milk Shakes

2 cups cold milk
1 package (4-serving size) JELL-O
  Instant Pudding and Pie Filling,
  any flavor
1 pint ice cream, any flavor
  Club soda

POUR milk into blender. Add pudding mix and ice cream; cover. Blend at high speed 30 seconds. Scrape sides of container; blend 30 seconds longer. Pour into glasses. Top with club soda. Serve immediately.

*MAKES about 5 cups
or 4 to 6 servings*

Prep time: 5 minutes

■ Easy Pudding Milk Shakes

3 cups cold milk
1 package (4-serving size) JELL-O
  Instant Pudding and Pie Filling,
  any flavor
1½ cups ice cream, any flavor

POUR milk into blender. Add pudding mix and ice cream; cover. Blend at high speed 30 seconds or until smooth. Pour into glasses. Serve immediately. (Mixture thickens as it stands. Thin with additional milk, if desired.)

*MAKES about 5 cups
or 4 to 6 servings*

Prep time: 5 minutes

■ Fruit Flavor Milk Shakes

2 cups cold milk
1 package (4-serving size) JELL-O
  Brand Gelatin, any flavor
1 pint vanilla ice cream

POUR milk into blender. Add gelatin and ice cream; cover. Blend at high speed 30 seconds or until smooth. Pour into glasses. *MAKES about 4 cups
or 4 servings*

Prep time: 5 minutes

Clockwise from top: Fruit Flavor Milk Shakes; Frosty Pudding Milk Shakes; Easy Pudding Milk Shakes

■ Gelatin Shots (Nonalcoholic)

1 package (4-serving size) JELL-O
   Brand Gelatin, any flavor
1 cup boiling water
1 cup cold liquid (see variations
   below)

DISSOLVE gelatin in boiling water. Add cold liquid. Pour into 12 (2-ounce) souffle cups. Chill until set, about 1 hour.   *MAKES 12 servings*

Cherry Cola Shots: Use cherry flavor gelatin and cola beverage.

Creamy Orange Shots: Use orange flavor gelatin. Substitute 1 cup vanilla ice cream for cold liquid.

Gingerberry Shots: Use raspberry or strawberry flavor gelatin and ginger ale.

Tangy Peach Shots: Use peach flavor gelatin. Substitute 1 container (8 ounces) peach or vanilla yogurt for cold liquid.

Sunshine Shots: Dissolve 1 package (4-serving size) orange flavor gelatin in 1 cup boiling water; add 1 cup cold sparkling water. Repeat with 1 package (4-serving size) strawberry flavor gelatin. Pour orange gelatin into 24 (2-ounce) souffle cups, filling each cup halfway. Chill until almost set, about 20 minutes. Pour strawberry gelatin over orange gelatin in cups. Chill until set, about 1 hour. Makes 24 servings.

Prep time: 10 minutes
Chill time: 1 hour

■ Easy Eggnog

2 packages (4-serving size each)
   JELL-O Instant Pudding and Pie
   Filling, French Vanilla or Vanilla
   Flavor
2 quarts cold milk
2 quarts cold prepared eggnog
1 cup brandy, rum or orange
   liqueur

COMBINE pudding mix with 2 cups of the milk; stir until slightly thickened. Stir in remaining 6 cups milk and eggnog until well blended. Stir in brandy. Chill until ready to serve. Top with whipped topping and sprinkle with nutmeg, if desired.   *MAKES about 18 cups or 36 servings*

Prep time: 10 minutes

INDEX